Sharing
the Gospel
of Salvation

Second Edition

CHURCH HOUSE
PUBLISHING

THE ARCHBISHOP
OF CANTERBURY

Church House Publishing
Church House
Great Smith Street
London SW1P 3AZ

ISBN 978 1 78140 159 0 (PB)
ISBN 978 1 78140 160 6 (Kindle Edition)
ISBN 978 1 78140 161 3 (Core Source eBook)

The first edition of *Sharing the Gospel of Salvation*
was published by the Archbishops' Council in 2010.

This revised and expanded edition was published 2019
by Church House Publishing
Copyright © The Archbishops' Council 2010, 2019

Scripture quotations are from the New Revised Standard
Version of the Bible, Anglicized Edition, copyright © 1989,
1995 by the Division of Christian Education of the National
Council of the Churches of Christ in the USA. Used by
permission. All rights reserved.

Printed and bound in England by Ashford Colour Press

Contents

Introduction

by Archbishop Justin Welby

In 2010, the General Synod of the Church of England published *Sharing the Gospel of Salvation*. This report was produced in response to a Private Member's Motion seeking a commitment to evangelism in the midst of the diverse claims of other religious traditions. *Sharing the Gospel of Salvation* affirmed the witness of the Church to the finality of Jesus Christ and commended the ministry and mission of churches to that end.

The report provided a theological and historical overview, rooting the Church of England's mandate of witness and proclamation in the heart of the global and historic Church. It reminded us that the Church of England was itself a product of that missionary instinct to share the good news of Jesus Christ. Evangelism, along with prayer and reconciliation, is a core priority during my time as Archbishop of Canterbury and it is appropriate that the 2010 General Synod report is revisited and revised for a new and wider audience.

In revising *Sharing the Gospel of Salvation*, it is my hope that the wisdom and theological resourcing offered here will enable churches to have confidence in their calling to evangelism to all faiths and none, coupled with an awareness of the sensitivities that must be navigated. The original Foreword by my predecessor Archbishop Rowan Williams and Archbishop John Sentamu acknowledged that the core principles for evangelism among those without a religious tradition are relevant also to those with a religious tradition, albeit that they may be applied differently because of the particularities of history and context. We are not in the business of selling a product or competing for power and prestige. Good evangelism does not manipulate or exploit, but stems from a wholehearted concern for the other in love, whether they decide to respond to the work of the Holy Spirit to conversion or not.

What is apparent, though, are the depths of cultural and religious sensitivities that can be at play when Christians witness to those of another tradition. The significance of colonial history casting a shadow on so many Anglican relations with other faiths should not be underestimated. So, alongside case studies, a sense of history and social context are integral to the resource offered in *Sharing the Gospel of Salvation*. It is no coincidence that the case studies all underline the importance of relationship: of consistent living and working alongside other religious traditions. The gospel of salvation is understood and received in the context of communities of Christians modelling service, repentance and forgiveness, celebration, worship and prayer.

The Church of England's Presence and Engagement programme seeks to resource those churches with at least 10% of parishioners from another religious tradition. Its mandate was renewed by General Synod in 2017 with one of its stated aims for the next five years being 'that churches become confident in sharing the gospel sensitively and effectively with people from other backgrounds, and in welcoming those who embrace Christian faith'. The reality is that evangelism is not a standalone activity that exists as the flip-side of dialogue. Confidence in sharing the gospel comes from a profound listening to the needs of our surrounding communities. Sensitivity to other backgrounds in that sharing requires that we are attentive to fears that they may feel they are only cared for as 'evangelism-fodder'.

There is some truth in the caricature that has dogged the perception of 'interfaith': a false binary between dialogue that assumed fundamentally shared values and beliefs, and evangelism that saw proclamation to those of other faiths as the only valid encounter in mission. As I visit churches, I am encouraged to see increasing evidence of gatherings for dialogue that take seriously key differences between faiths. These meetings of people from different faiths are addressing difficult and challenging topics in interreligious relations, including the issues sometimes provoked by conversion. Similarly, it is heartening when I hear of churches that have typically committed to evangelism but also found themselves serving people of other faith traditions in very practical ways and even developing meetings for greater mutual understanding in dialogue. These developments are a reminder of an essential truth of Christian theology: as we turn outwards to the world in prayerful ways, rooted in our traditions of bible reading, worship and eucharist, we too should expect to be transformed. There is a schooling in sharing the gospel, especially with those of other faiths, where we can expect to find Christ as much as proclaim Christ.

Our challenge is not whether to witness to the gospel of salvation with those of other faiths but how our church communities model and affirm genuine good news so that our words explain our deeds, and our deeds support our words. Evangelism, work for the common good, and dialogue are not three competing and contradictory activities for the Church but integral aspects of mission.

In revising the original *Sharing the Gospel of Salvation*, some updates in terms of social context, recommended reading and statistics have been made, noting the more recent 2011 census data that is now available.

The case studies have been reframed as 'snapshots', recognizing the ongoing significance of the stories of some of these churches while allowing for subsequent changes in project direction, funding schemes and personnel.

In the revised Concluding Reflections, the report observes the recent phenomenon of significant numbers of converts from Islam among the Persian diaspora in Britain. This development alerts us to the need to develop liturgical and catechetical resources that are responsive to different cultures, as well as the importance of encouraging leaders from different backgrounds. As we share the gospel of salvation among people of all faiths and none, my expectation and prayer is that the Church itself will be challenged to change as we discover anew the fullness of Christ in our diverse world.

✠ JUSTIN CANTUAR

Foreword to the First Edition of 2010

by Archbishop Rowan Williams
and Archbishop John Sentamu

The gospel testifies to the uniqueness of Jesus Christ in God's plan for the salvation of the world. There can be no greater theme – and no higher calling for the Church – than to bear witness to salvation in and through Christ. One might think that any attempt to address a matter of such magnitude in the thin pages of a Synod report is sure to be inadequate and, indeed, there is much that this report does not, and cannot do. Nevertheless, it is a timely and important report because it addresses the day-to-day impact of Christian doctrine on the life of the Church and our relationship with the people and cultures around us.

There is often a gap between the great declarations of Christian doctrine and the practical outworking of belief in the daily discipleship of Christian men and women and the communities they create and inhabit. The gap is not so much one of inconsistency but one of understanding the connections. The Church in every age must give close attention to how it lives as a neighbour among others, and how such neighbourliness is informed and shaped by its overarching beliefs about the nature of God and Christ's transformation of the world. This report is a bridge between what we believe about God's saving work in Christ and the practical implications for discipleship in a world made profoundly complex and confusing by rapid change and a deepening appreciation of social, cultural and religious plurality.

When Mr Paul Eddy moved the Private Member's Motion at General Synod in 2009, which led to this report, he was supported, both on the platform and in the debate itself, by Synod members from right across the range of doctrine and practice within the Church of England. That breadth of support exemplified how the Church of England is strongly united in its commitment to the unique revelation of God in Jesus Christ.

How, then, shall we share this amazing gift with the people around us? This is where a note of uncertainty sometimes creeps in. In a society fixated on personal choice, it is sometimes, paradoxically, frowned upon to promote one's own choices as good for others. Our society is also acutely alert to instances of the abuse of power, and this sensitivity is greatly to be welcomed. It also makes us – rightly – alert to abuses of power perpetrated by the Church, as well as to the social inequalities that make people vulnerable to the power of others today. The stronger sense of difference and diversity – including religious diversity – in Britain today has challenged us to become a more generous culture. Sadly, it has also made many nervous of publicly espousing a vision of the common good for all people. Yet, if the Good News of God in Christ is good for us, how can we refrain from commending it as good for others too?

Sharing the Gospel of Salvation makes two helpful points in this respect. First, it reminds the Church of its history in relation to other cultures around it. It was the desire to share the gift of God in Christ that brought the Christian faith to Britain, and it is that same desire that has renewed the Church through the centuries as it has come into contact with the insights, wisdom and challenges of others. The Church's history of mission, like all long histories, has its shadow side. The call to mission, when allied with political or economic power, has sometimes led to actions in Christ's name that have been inconsistent with Christ's own teaching. When evangelism and political dominance become intertwined there are always problems. But the fear of getting it wrong should never obscure the Christian's commitment to the good of all and to making Christ the centrepiece of that good. Too much reticence is as untrue to our history and our vocation today as was the cultural insensitivity of an earlier age. There is much to be thankful for in the faithful and sacrificial work and witness of two centuries or more of Anglican missions, most notably in the work of the mission societies, particularly where they have been ready to serve the priorities of the indigenous church.

Second, the report provides a salutary warning of just how dominant the language of the market – of choice, consumption and marketing – has become in our culture. Markets are a key part of a free and prosperous society. But they can never provide all that is needed to secure wellbeing and happiness. A confusion between mission and marketing is understandable but unhelpful.

Christ's saving work is not a commodity to be sold but a gift to be shared. If we keep always in mind the central insight that it is not we who bring others to Christ but God working in them, we can avoid colluding with the marketing mindset that would paint every evangelist as a huckster and portray God's children as 'targets' for conversion. When our encounters with our neighbours, of other faiths and none, are distinguished from exercises in salesmanship, we can be confident that we are sharing God's love rather than marketing another lifestyle choice.

But what does this mean in practice? A large part of this report is drawn from the work of parishes, clergy and lay people living out their discipleship, many in areas where, as in the early days of the Church, Christians live as citizens alongside large numbers of people of other faiths. The report places each example in its social context and goes on to show what real churches and real Christians are doing to proclaim Christ among their neighbours.

Because we share our humanity and citizenship with others, there is much common activity across differences of faith and religion. The best work recognizes that, because we are Christians, our understanding of the good and our reasons for pursuing the good in real-life situations are grounded in the reality of Jesus Christ – and we must be entirely up front about that source of our commitment.

The experience of parishes and people working in multi faith contexts is that, while stridency is counterproductive, failure to be open about our beliefs is equally unhelpful. Others want to know why we do things as well as seeing what we do. Because God loves all His people, encounters begin with respect for the other. If we are too cautious of sharing openly the foundations of our beliefs and the nature of our discipleship – if we hold back the most important aspect of our motivation – we put constraints on that respect and deny a little of God's nature.

A word that has become most contentious is conversion. It is certainly a word that for some carries some unfortunate connotations. God's offer of salvation in Christ is not one consumer choice among others but a matter of profound importance to human identity and character. It is precisely because of this deep seriousness that, in a divided and unequal society, conversion can be perceived to carry with it the implication of betrayal – of extinguishing old identities and loyalties in which there was much that was good. Such sensitivies mean that our language of conversion must be generous and handled with care.

But conversion must never become a word of which Christians fight shy. In Christ, old identities are never the last word and the good is offered for all the world. So there should be nothing embarrassed or awkward about the Church's commitment to draw others to Christ. This we do, not in order to win favour for ourselves, nor to make others more like us, for indeed we may be challenged and changed in the process, but simply because we want to share God's gifts as we have received them – freely and unearned.

If this feels like a delicate path to tread with integrity – and it often is – the guidelines for good practice developed from experience, and offered in this report, make clear that it is far from impossible. Indeed, within these pages there are many inspiring stories of parishes and people who have made it happen, and happen well.

God reaches out in Christ to people everywhere. Christ is, for us, the final and unique revelation of what is good for all humanity. Together, as the Church, we seek to live more like Christ, offering ourselves wholly and selflessly in pursuit of the good of all. This report gives us good examples and guidelines for doing just that, among people of other faiths and none, in a society more fluid and complex by far than most previous generations had to contend with. We commend this report. It is not the last word on the Church's practice in mission and evangelism, but it emphasizes rightly that, for the Church, Christ is indeed the last – and the first – Word.

✠ ROWAN CANTUAR

✠ SENTAMU EBOR

1 Sharing the Gospel of Salvation – Background

In February 2009, the General Synod debated a Private Member's Motion from Mr Paul Eddy which, after amendment, was passed in the following terms by an overwhelming majority:

> That this Synod warmly welcome Dr Martin Davie's background paper 'The witness of Scripture, the Fathers and the historic formularies to the uniqueness of Christ' attached to GS Misc 905B and request the House of Bishops to report to the Synod on their understanding of the uniqueness of Christ in Britain's multi-faith society, and offer examples and commendations of good practice in sharing the gospel of salvation through Christ alone with people of other faiths and of none.

Following the Group of Sessions, the House of Bishops nominated two bishops to convene a group that would be responsible for taking the motion forward. The group consisted of the Rt Revd Pete Broadbent, the Rt Revd Paul Williams, the Rt Revd Dr Toby Howarth, the Revd Dr Malcolm Brown, the Revd Canon Guy Wilkinson, and Dr Martin Davie.

Responding to the motion has not been an easy task – mainly because the motion encompasses so many potential themes. In one sense, the only adequate response to the motion is to present the whole gamut of the Church's work in mission and evangelism, since the scope of our outreach to 'people of other faiths and none' embraces all the outward-facing activities of the Christian Church.

We have, however, deliberately restricted the scope of our work to make it manageable. We recognize that there are major areas of specialized apologetics that we have not attempted to cover: for example, presenting the claims of Christ, the Kingdom and the gospel in the context of the strident atheism currently focussing its arguments on a presumed incompatibility between 'science' and 'religion'. We know that a forthcoming Diocesan Synod Motion will allow proper attention to be given to this specific question.

Our focus, by contrast, has tried to reflect the course of the Synod debate by addressing first the question of proclaiming the uniqueness of Christ among people who are already committed to faith, usually as an adherent of one of the great world religions. As we note below, it is important to distinguish the major world faiths from the religious belief systems that the Church classifies as New Religious Movements, and to distinguish both from belief systems that do not regard themselves as religions or faiths. While many of the points in our report can be translated to the second and third of these contexts, we did not believe that we could do justice to all three when the questions arising in the first context were so complex, pressing, and of concern to Synod.

Our report begins with a brief summary of the unique significance of Jesus Christ that draws on the work produced by Martin Davie for the General Synod debate last February. It then gives a brief overview of the Church of England's mission activity among those of other religions, showing that such activity has always been a feature of the life of the English

Church. After that it looks at the social and religious context for mission
and evangelism today and sets out some guidance for 'good practice'
in sharing the gospel of salvation through Christ. The guidance on
good practice builds on the experience of a number of case studies
presented in the first edition of the report which demonstrate some
of the potentials and pitfalls of work in this field, with much to celebrate
and much to learn from.

In reflecting on the case studies that were used in the first edition of the
report and more contemporary case studies in the light of the theology
and social context explored earlier, we offer some guidelines for mission
and evangelism among people of other faiths (much of which can be
developed for use among people of no faith). These guidelines have
been drawn from the experience of the many practitioners with whom
we have been in contact for both published editions. We commend these
reflections to the Church as tools for enhancing the work of proclaiming
Christ to the nation.

In compiling this report, the group is indebted to the many colleagues
and contacts who have shared their work with us and assisted in the
development of our thinking. While the content of the report is our
responsibility alone, we could not have completed it without the
enthusiastic support and generous sharing of time and expertise that
we have enjoyed from others. In particular, we have learned much from
the *Presence and Engagement* project, sponsored on behalf of Synod
by the Mission and Public Affairs Division, and from many who have

taken part in that work. In addition, we would like to thank: the Revd Dale Barton, the Revd Dave Bookless, the Rt Revd John Goddard, the Revd Jay Macleod, Dr Andrew Smith and the Revd Dr Richard Sudworth and the very many others who work with them.

2   The Unique Significance of Jesus Christ

The basis for the Christian Church's understanding of the unique significance of Jesus Christ lies in the affirmation of the oneness of God which is found in the Old Testament in passages such as the following:

> To you it was shown so that you would acknowledge that the Lord is God; there is no other besides him. Deuteronomy 4.35

> And Ezra said: 'You are the Lord, you alone; you have made heaven, the heaven of heavens, with all their host, the earth and all that is on it, the seas and all that is in them. To all of them you give life, and the host of heaven worships you.' Nehemiah 9.6

> I am the Lord, and there is no other; besides me there is no God;
> I arm you, though you do not know me, so that they may know from the rising of the sun and from the west, that there is no one besides me; I am the Lord, and there is no other. Isaiah 45.5–6

In passages such as these, and in its overall storyline, the Old Testament teaches that the Lord, the God of Israel, the God of Abraham, Isaac and Jacob is unique as 'the one living and true God' (Article I). It is he who has created and who upholds the universe and everything that exists within it and he is the sole ruler of history.

On the basis of Jesus' teaching about himself and his mission and on the basis of his life, death, resurrection and ascension, the first Christians came to believe that, in accordance with the promises that he had made to his people, the God of Israel, in the person of Jesus, 'took Man's nature in the womb of the blessed Virgin, of her substance' (Article II) in order to proclaim God's kingdom and to bring it in by reconciling the whole universe through his life, death and resurrection. They also held that after his resurrection Jesus ascended into heaven and at the end of the age he will come in glory to judge the living and the dead and to finally and fully manifest the kingly rule of God over all of creation.

The first Christians therefore believed that Jesus was God incarnate. This belief can be seen in passages such as:

> John 1.14: And the Word became flesh and lived among us, and we have seen his glory, the glory as of a father's only son, full of grace and truth.

> Colossians 1.19–20: For in him all the fullness of God was pleased to dwell, and through him God was pleased to reconcile to himself all things, whether on earth or in heaven, by making peace through the blood of his cross.

> Hebrews 1.1–3: Long ago God spoke to our ancestors in many and various ways by the prophets, but in these last days he has spoken to us by a Son, whom he appointed heir of all things, through whom he also created the worlds. He is the reflection of God's glory and the exact imprint of God's very being, and he sustains all things by his powerful word.

Although the first Christians believed that Jesus was divine they did not believe that God was simply Jesus. On the basis of the same evidence that had led them to believe that Jesus was God they also believed that God exists also as the Father, the one to whom Jesus prayed, to whom Jesus was obedient, who raised Jesus from the dead and to whom Jesus would hand over the kingdom at the end of time. On the same grounds, they further believed that God exists as the Holy Spirit, the one who had dwelt in Jesus and empowered his mission and whom Jesus had poured out on his followers on the day of Pentecost.

The first Christians thus redefined the Old Testament belief in the oneness of God, holding that the Lord, the one God of Israel, exists as the Father, the Son who had become incarnate in Jesus and as the Holy Spirit. This redefinition can be seen in passages such as 1 Corinthians 8.6: 'For us there is one God, the Father, from whom are all things and for whom we exist, and one Lord, Jesus Christ, through whom are all things and through whom we exist'; and Ephesians 4.4–6:

> 'There is one body and one Spirit, just as you were called to the one hope of your calling, one Lord, one faith, one baptism, one God and Father of all, who is above all and through all and in all.'

Where the first Christians led, the Church of the Patristic period followed. When in the early centuries of the Church's existence people called into question the full deity of the Son or the Spirit or the true humanity of Jesus the Church re-affirmed both in the Apostles, Nicene and Athanasian Creeds and in the Chalcedonian definition.

As a church that belongs to 'the One, Holy Catholic and Apostolic Church worshipping the one true God, Father, Son and Holy Spirit' and professing 'the faith uniquely revealed in the Holy Scriptures and set forth in the catholic creeds' (Canon C.15), the Church of England follows the lead of the first Christians and the Church of the Patristic period. It bears witness in its historic formularies to the God who is Father, Son and Holy Spirit and who became incarnate in Jesus. It is this God whom it proclaims in its mission and evangelism. It is this God in whose name it baptizes people.

It is its faith in this God that is also the basis for the Church of England's engagement with people of all religions and none. It believes that the God it confesses is the source of salvation that is offered to all people everywhere (whether they are yet aware of the fact or not), and the ultimate source of the values that it shares in common with them. But it also holds that, in obedience to the commission given by Jesus to his disciples (Matt. 28.18–20; Acts 1.8), all Christians are called to act as God's instruments in bringing people to explicit faith in Jesus Christ and to membership of his Church through baptism.[1]

---

[1] For a more detailed account of the issue covered in this theological summary see M. Davie, *A Church of England Approach to the Unique Significance of Jesus Christ*, Crowther Centre Monographs, 7, Oxford: Church Mission Society, 2009.

3 The History of the English Church's Missionary Activity Among Those of Other Religions

Because those who have belonged to the Church in England have believed in the unique significance of Jesus Christ in the context of the Trinitarian understanding of God just described, a consistent feature of the life of the Church in England has been the desire to share faith in Christ with those of other religions.

We do not have precise information about how or when the earliest conversions to Christianity took place in Roman Britain, but in the nature of the case these conversions must have involved Christians sharing the gospel with non-Christians and these non-Christians then accepting Christianity in place of one of the many other forms of religious belief prevalent in the later Roman Empire. It is important, in the current debate about the Church sharing its faith with people of other religions, to remember that the very roots of the Church of England lie in this process taking place. The Church in England is passing on, as it has always done, what it first received from others.

If we move on to those periods for which we do have information, we find that the Church in what became England sought for and achieved the conversion of first the Anglo-Saxons and then the Vikings to Christianity and that this conversion involved an acceptance of Christianity in place of their ancestral religion.

The same pattern can also be seen in the case of the missionary work undertaken in the seventh and eighth centuries in Frisia (what is now north-western Germany and the Netherlands) by members of the English Church such as St Wilfrid of Ripon and St Boniface. In this case also conversion to Christianity from ancestral religion was sought and achieved.

By the later Anglo-Saxon period and throughout the Middle Ages, England was an almost entirely Christian country on the edge of a largely Christian continent. This meant that English Christians had very limited opportunities to undertake missionary activity among those of other religions. However, attempts were made to convert members of the small Jewish community in England and there are records of conversions from Judaism continuing to take place even after the Jewish community as a whole was expelled from England in 1290. In the fifteenth century, for example, we find the case of Sir Edward Brampton, a Portuguese Jew who came to England and was converted to Christianity, taking the name Edward after his godfather King Edward IV.

Sadly, it has to be acknowledged that in the conversion of Jewish people to Christianity there was often explicit or implicit coercion against a background of anti-Jewish polemic. This does not, however, mean that all conversions were a result of coercion and that converts such as Edward Brampton never freely chose to embrace the Christian faith.

During the Middle Ages Christians from England were also involved in the Crusades. The Crusades were not examples of mission in that they were never intended to convert the Muslim world and the motives of those who took part in them were often secular as well as religious.

Nevertheless, the significance of the Crusades for Christian mission needs to be acknowledged since the fear and mistrust between Christians and Muslims that were a legacy of the Crusades have continued to overshadow Christian-Muslim relations and Christian mission among Muslim people to the present day.

With the opening up of global communications in the fifteenth century the opportunities for more extensive missionary work among adherents of other religions opened up as well and from the seventeenth century onwards the Church of England came to recognize these opportunities and to try to take advantage of them. Thus the charter given to the Virginia Company in 1606 to found a new colony on the east coast of North America included the intention of 'propagating the Christian religion' and a chaplain was appointed for the purpose and the provision of a service of adult baptism in the 1662 revision of the *Book of Common Prayer* was stated to be 'useful for the baptizing of the natives of our plantations and others converted to the faith'.

As in the cases of Jewish conversion noted earlier, the propagation of Christianity in the context of slavery and colonialism was often problematic, and the motives of those involved were often mixed. Nevertheless, a key point to note here is that it was assumed that the gospel of Jesus Christ was for everyone, of whatever religious or ethnic background, and that everyone had the right to become part of the Church through baptism.

The end of the seventeenth century saw the foundation of the Society for the Propagation of Christian Knowledge (SPCK) and the Society for the Propagation of the Gospel (SPG), both of which supported and undertook overseas missionary activity among those of other faiths. These two bodies were the precursors of a series of other Church of England voluntary missionary societies that developed during the eighteenth, nineteenth and twentieth centuries with the same intention. The overseas missionary work of the Church of England-based mission societies has continued to the present day and their experience of engagement with people of other faiths is a resource on which the Church of England continues to draw.

During the eighteenth and most of the nineteenth centuries missionary activity among those of other religions was seen as something that needed to take place overseas (the presence of those of other religions in England being still very small), but with the growth of large scale Jewish immigration into England in the nineteenth century the Church of England undertook renewed missionary work among the Jewish community in England, this work being led by the London Society for Promoting Christianity Among the Jews (what is now the Church's Ministry Among Jewish People, the CMJ). The twentieth century saw continuing Jewish immigration to this country. Latterly there has also been large scale immigration by those of other major world religions as well.[1]

What this brief historical survey shows is that there is nothing new or abnormal about members of the Church of England bearing witness to members of other religions in the hope that this will lead to them to

---

[1] It should be noted that there has also been Christian immigration into this country from Africa, Asia and the West Indies and elsewhere.

come to faith and be baptized. On the contrary, it is something that Christians in this country have sought to do throughout the history of the Church in England. What would be abnormal would be for members of the Church of England to stop seeking to share their faith in this way.

The history of the involvement of members of the Church in England in mission has its dark side. The motives of those involved in mission have sometimes been mixed, the methods that have been used have not always been ones of which we would approve today and at times there has been an unhealthy connection between mission and colonialism. However, this ambiguous history is not a reason for members of the Church of England to give up on mission. Rather, it should be an incentive to try to ensure that our mission is always rooted in love for God and for our neighbours from other faiths and is undertaken in a way that appropriately reflects this love.

4   The Social Context of Mission and Evangelism Today

Post War Change

In 1945, taking stock and seeking new directions after a cataclysmic World War, the Church of England published a major report on mission and evangelism – *Towards the Conversion of England.* In many ways, the report now reads as if it came out of another world. Not only was the process – involving a working party of 50 people, including five bishops – unwieldy by today's standards, but the 'mental atmosphere' of the whole report is redolent of a world in which Christians (and especially the Church of England) saw themselves called to define and embody the moral framework of the nation and able to call upon national institutions of all kinds to reinforce the Church's message.

Other Christian churches and denominations are virtually invisible within the report's 172 pages, and the ethnic homogeneity of the English is simply taken for granted. The only reference to other faiths is the comment that the 'Person and Character of Christ' was the element in Christianity that 'appealed most to the Mohammedans in Persia.'[1]

The proper twenty-first-century reaction to the report's strangeness is not mockery but the realization that the social landscape that we take

---

[1] *Towards the Conversion of England:* The Archbishop's Commission on Evangelism, London: Press and Publications Board of the Church Assembly, 1945, para. 79.

as given is, in fact, extremely recent in terms of human experience and memory. Our current members over the age of 80 would have grown up in the world portrayed by the report, and many more, though younger, would have recognized and owned the context through much of their life as disciples. An understanding of the rapidity of social change is just the first step towards developing strategies for addressing it – and evaluating such strategies in the light of experience takes even longer.

Towards the Conversion of England addressed a degree of apathy and ignorance about the Christian faith that was perceived as new in England, but the character of English citizens was seen as a constant. Although the report explored theological issues to some extent, it was mainly with the purpose of reaffirming conventional pre-War understandings. The report addressed mission in ways that suggested that the great majority of the population remained residually Christian in their moral formation. The extent to which foundational Christian narratives have faded from the collective memory, as well as the diversity of the people of our communities, are newer factors where the church has much less experience and engagement.

The Profile of Religion in Britain Today (2011)

Religion (2011 census)

	Number (million)	Per cent of population
Christian	33,243	59.3
No religion	14,097	25.1
Muslim	2,706	4.8
Hindu	817	1.5
Sikh	423	0.8
Jewish	263	0.5
Buddhist	248	0.4
Other	241	0.4
Not stated	4,038	7.2

Source: Office of National Statistics. Figures from 2011 census.[2]

When the first edition of Sharing the Gospel of Salvation was published in 2010, the statistics for religious affiliation, drawing from the 2001 census, were represented as follows:

---

[2] www.ons.gov.uk/peoplepopulationandcommunity/culturalidentity/religion/articles/religioninenglandandwales2011/2012-12-11 (accessed 14.12.2018).

Population of England and Wales: By Religion (April 2001)

Non-Christian

	Total population		Religious population
	Numbers	Percentages	Percentages
Christian	41,014,811	71.8	
Muslim	1,588,890	2.8	51.9
Hindu	558,342	1.0	18.3
Sikh	336,179	0.6	11.0
Jewish	267,373	0.5	8.7
Buddhist	149,157	0.3	4.9
Other religion	159,167	0.3	5.2
All non-Christian Religious pop.	3,059,108	5.4	100.0
No religion	8,596,488	15.1	
Religion not stated	4,433,520	7.8	
All population	57,103,927		100.0

Source: Office of National Statistics. Figures from 2001 census.[3]

---

[3] www.statistics.gov.uk/cci/nugget.asp?id=954 (accessed 15.9.2009).

The changes in number and proportion show a startling decline in self-identification as 'Christian', a growing assertion of 'no belief' and a rise in the proportion of the Muslim population. The Christian percentage has decreased between 2001 and 2011 from 71.8% to 59.3%. While the figures for Christianity tend to disguise the reality of allegiance and attendance manifest in the cultural shift from nominal identification with the Christian faith to a post-Christendom context, the trajectory is unarguable. Several of the other religious groups are growing as a proportion of the overall population with the most marked increase being those who identify as Muslim: from 2.8% to 4.8%. The proportion is still a small one in national terms.

The national picture might suggest an overall decline in the significance of religion in the population, but the local stories reveal much greater complexity. Our urban centres are in fact places of significant religiosity.

Local Authorities with the Highest Proportions of Main Minority
Religious Groups (2011)

England and Wales

	Percentages		Percentages
Muslim		**Jewish**	
Tower Hamlets	34.5	Barnet	15.2
Newham	32.0	Hertsmere	14.3
Blackburn with Darwen	27.0	Hackney	6.3
Bradford	24.7	Bury	5.6
Luton	24.6	Camden	4.5
Hindu		**Buddhist**	
Harrow	25.3	Rushmoor	3.3
Brent	17.8	Greenwich	1.7
Leicester	15.2	Kensington and Chelsea	1.5
Redbridge	11.4	Westminster	1.5
Hounslow	10.3	Hounslow	1.4
Sikh			
Slough	10.6		
Wolverhampton	9.1		
Hounslow	9.0		
Sandwell	8.7		
Ealing	7.9		

Source: Census 2011, Office for National Statistics.[4]

_____

[4] www.ons.gov.uk/peoplepopulationandcommunity/culturalidentity/religion/
articles/religioninenglandandwales2011/2012-12-11 (accessed 14.12.2018).

As the 2010 report affirmed, religious affiliations in Britain are not geographically uniform. The trend is not towards an increasing secularization but processes of religious resurgence in some areas, and religious decline in others. For increasing numbers of Church of England communicants, though, their lived reality will involve daily encounters in friendship, neighbourhoods and work-life with adherents of other faiths, especially in our larger towns and cities.

Grace Davie characterizes the actual complexity as the 'persistent paradox' of Britain's religiosity. There are trends that go in opposing directions: of decreasing religiosity, both in terms of numbers and levels of commitment, and growing religious plurality and a more vivid public profile to religion.[5] The enhanced profile of religious discourse is something that Davie recognizes as over-inflating the underlying reality of religious allegiance. Thus, she can say that 'other-faith populations are growing in this country, but two points must be kept firmly in mind: these communities – though expanding – are both modest in size and varied in nature'.[6] This is an essential context to this report, where the Church should not be tempted to ape some of the media over-inflation of the impact of other religions that Davie observes.

London, perhaps unsurprisingly, is the most religiously diverse city in the country but also has the smallest proportion of non-religious.[7] In what

---

[5] G. Davie, *Religion in Britain: A Persistent Paradox*, Oxford: Wiley-Blackwell, 2015.
[6] Davie, *Religion in Britain*, p. 15.
[7] Davie, *Religion in Britain*, pp. 43–4.

are now commonly described as 'super-diverse' cities such as London and Birmingham, religious diversity is normative. The context to which *Sharing the Gospel of Salvation* speaks is a Britain of huge variety and diversity, where religious diversity in many neighbourhoods is an everyday reality, while for some in other areas there is minimal diversity. What is clear, though, is that the public profile of other religions in Britain has risen, with Islam arguably having a disproportionate presence in the media.

History and Faiths in Britain Today

It has been argued that the notion of religious uniformity in Britain ended in 1689 with the Act of Toleration which allowed freedom of worship to Trinitarian Protestant Dissenters. From that point, and especially after the Catholic Relief Act of 1829, religious practice very gradually became a matter of individual conscience rather than an integral element of national identity and loyalty to the Crown. The principle of religious toleration largely involved toleration of diversity among Christians. Diversity between faiths, principally the gradual accommodation of the Jewish community in Britain, was – perhaps paradoxically – less contested and therefore made less of an impact on thinking. Certainly, in the nineteenth century, the notion that Englishness required complete religious conformity was radically upset.

Adherents of faiths other than Christianity have been present in Britain for centuries, but so long as they remained tiny minorities they were simultaneously perceived as exceptional and too small to be publicly visible except where substantial immigrant populations had tended to live close together over several generations. Successive waves of migration, especially since the Second World War from Commonwealth countries, have multiplied the number of such communities and widened the number of faiths that are publicly visible to all.

It is worth noting that, while religious adherence and ethnicity are not the same thing, the visibility of many ethnic groups has often been conflated in popular thinking with religious diversity. The fact that, for example, Christianity in Britain is extremely diverse in ethnic terms has not significantly dented this tendency to conflate ethnicity and faith.

The twentieth century assumption that religion is a matter of individual conscience, confined in many respects to the private sphere, is strongly challenged by the presence of religious groups that are closely associated with visibly distinctive ethnic groups. Contemporary British attitudes to religion have not fully assimilated this shift.

Although the teleology of ecumenical and inter faith encounter is radically different, there may be lessons to be learned in the multi faith context from our experience of Christian ecumenism. In particular, ecumenism required close attention to theology, to the history of intolerance, and to present inequalities in size and resources between churches. Negotiating these factors was (and remains) frustrating and time-consuming, but necessary if the churches' theology of engagement was to develop authentically.

However, looking beyond the churches to national policies regarding faith communities, these sensitivities seem often to be lacking. A 2008 report noted the lack of direct experience and understanding of any religious tradition among government ministers and senior civil servants.[8] An All Party Parliamentary Group on Religious Education in 2016 concluded that 'the Civil Service, other parts of the public sector and the media as being particular priority areas where religious literacy needs to be improved'.[9] This may explain why religions and faith communities are so frequently portrayed as essentially problematic, as equivalent to one another over and against a default secularism, and equal treatment is often interpreted in ways that ignore historic and present differences.

What is often not appreciated by government, both national and local, and by many in the public sector, is the request regularly expressed by faith leaders from the great world faiths that Christians should speak authentically and clearly about our understanding of our faith, and that the country is best served, not by Christians downplaying our religious heritage, but by the public expression of Christian faith and practice in schools and other public institutions. Many of our other faith partners wish us to be unashamedly Christian.

It is too simple to assume a straightforward shift in culture from a position of a national Christian identity to a 'multi faith' community in

---

[8] F. Davis, E. Paulhaus and A. Bradstock, *Moral, but no Compass: Government, Church and the Future of Welfare*, Chelmsford: Matthew James Publishing, 2008.
[9] All Party Parliamentary Group on Religious Education, July 2016, *Improving Religious Literacy: A Contribution to the Debate*, p. 49, www.reonline.org.uk/wp-content/uploads/2016/07/APPG-on-RE-Improving-Religious-Literacy-full-report.pdf (accessed 14.12.2018).

which a variety of faith positions relate to one another on a level playing field. In many ways, the metaphor of the market place, which is so pervasive in many aspects of our culture, encourages the erroneous notion that all religions and faith positions are of equal status and can compete with each other in a kind of spiritual free market. This view is ill-founded. The former dominance of Christian (and especially Anglican) norms in society places the Christian churches in a particular relationship to other faith communities which is not one of simple equivalence in the present. The historical role of Christianity in England is both an opportunity and a potential stumbling block to effective mission.

It is an opportunity because, however anxious some Christians may feel, they remain not only by far the largest practising religious group, but are by far the biggest group in the self-reported religious identity of English people. Life in Britain today means, for everyone, that some encounter with Christian ideas is inevitable (even if unconscious) and a full understanding of British institutions still requires some grasp of Christian thought.

But the historical fact of having once been a dominant feature of the social and political landscape is also a potential stumbling block to mission. The Church of England learned – sometimes painfully – how to work with other Christians in an increasingly secular context which affected them all. By extension, all Christians need similar skills in their relations with people of other faiths. Because being Christian and being British are often still conflated in the popular imagination, the political history of British attitudes and actions in other parts of the world, and toward people of other faiths, influences today's relationship between faith communities.

In this context, it is worth remembering that unhelpful associations between Christianity and prejudicial attitudes towards people who are 'different' are not quite dead. The far-right group, the English Defence League, use Christian rhetoric and the appropriation of the nation's Christian heritage in a culture war against the presence of Islam in Britain. There is a toxic mixture here of lingering colonial assumptions, racist attitudes, understandable anxieties and scapegoating of people who do not fit a narrow (and ahistorical) definition of British-ness. These attitudes are hard enough to disentangle from each other, and if they are then infused with Christian words and images the vulnerable groups against whom such rhetoric is directed may be forgiven for being confused about where Christians really stand.

Yet despite all the historical complexities, Christians are still called to preach the gospel to all creation, making disciples of all nations through the guidance and power of the Holy Spirit.[10] The Church's vocation is to go beyond tolerance into positive engagement and dialogue and change (tolerance having unfortunate overtones of indifference). The greatest challenge (numerically, at least) is still the indifference of many people to all notions of faith, and the pervasiveness of an essentially atheistic secularism as the default mode for understanding the social and human condition.

Among the objectives of mission, bringing people to faith, expressed in baptism, the catechumenate and discipleship, must always figure highly. But mission priorities are not set solely by the numerical challenge they

---

[10] For example in Acts 1.8; Luke 24.47–49; John 20.21; Mark 13.10.

represent. The church's reflections on mission and evangelism must encompass the diversity of religious and philosophical affiliations to be found in the nation as a whole. Social plurality is a reality (even if the impossibility of wide moral agreements is often overstated) and strategies for evangelization must be similarly multifaceted.

It is also worth recalling that Britain today remains a highly unequal and stratified society. In one sense we are a 'melting pot culture', but in other senses, the barriers that get in the way of friendly relationships are huge. As long as wealth and power are not only concentrated in few hands but are associated with specific social groupings, individual contact across the divides will be tainted by perceptions of inequality. Where disadvantage is felt disproportionately by some religious groups (who may experience compound disadvantage where religion, ethnicity, education and so on combine unfavourably) a great deal of trust-building is necessary to get beyond the barriers of inequality.

World Faiths, New Religious Movements and Secularism

It is sometimes helpful to use a three-fold model to look at the challenges posed to the church by the contemporary 'religious geography' of Britain. First, there are historic religions present both through the faith and practice of fellow British citizens and as global phenomena impacting on our understanding of ourselves as global citizens.

Second, there are the New Religious Movements and Alternative Spiritualities – bodies with shorter histories and arguably more recent cultural roots in contemporary society.

Third, there are the philosophies that are to some extent represented organizationally by two main bodies: the National Secular Society and the British Humanist Association. These bodies are relatively small in membership terms but claim to reflect the views of a much wider constituency.

The boundaries between these three groupings are contested (for instance, some pagans make the contested claim to be a more ancient religion in Britain than Christianity; some argue that the growth of NRMs is a by-product of secularization, etc.). However, the Church seeks to differentiate between these three categories which suggest something of the complexity of relationships within which the church's mission takes place.

One of the complexities of relating to other great world faiths is that, like Christianity itself, most faiths have an ongoing conversation between adherents about what it means to be a good member of that faith community. Christianity, like Islam, Judaism or other faiths with centuries of practice and politics behind them, is not one story, one set of practices or one structure of authority. Christian mission is not one set of practices either!

NRMs are too numerous to sum up in general terms, but some could be categorized as being derived from great world faiths. Jehovah's Witnesses, for instance, draw upon, even as they alter and add to, the central narratives of Christianity, and the Ahmadi community claims to Muslim identity are strongly contested by mainstream Islam. Others, such as Scientology, have no identifiable historical connections. These different lineages are important to bear in mind when discerning potential points of convergence and disagreement in the encounter with Christian missions.

The Gospel and its Reception

Many within the great world faiths will share disquiet about the dominance of secularist thinking in British society today. Not all, however, are agreed in their analysis of what is going on – it is not a simple matter of 'people of faith' versus 'secular humanism'. Differences of emphasis in relating to modernity are to be found within Christianity as within other faiths. For example, Christian theology is often quite comfortable with a modernist focus on the individual as moral agent which contrasts with the more strongly communitarian focus of pre-modern times.

Christianity has especially interesting complexities here, since the Enlightenment itself (often seen as the harbinger of contemporary secularism) developed in Christian Europe largely among people who saw Enlightenment values as the embodiment of Christian virtues. The relationship between the Enlightenment and the Reformation is fascinating, contentious and far too big a subject for this paper!

Other faiths may share an ambivalence about the fruits of the Enlightenment, but the tension is perhaps most acute among Christians. Some Christians involved in evangelism among Muslims note that the call to personal decision is overshadowed in Islamic history and culture by more communal understandings and a more communitarian Christian theology may be especially resonant as a tool of mission.

This takes us back to the comment in *Towards the Conversion of England* that some aspects of Christian theology are more easily communicable to Muslims than other doctrines. The wording of that report may be very dated, but the sentiment is important. Similar observations could be made about communicating Christian ideas to members of all other religions.

Towards the Conversion of England made many good points about how effective mission involves the simultaneous ability to speak the language of contemporary culture(s) and the ability to address the gaps that cultures ignore – the human longing expressed in the (often unspoken) question, 'there must be more to life than this'. The missioner or evangelist (on a Pauline model) must be fluent in the ways of contemporary cultures and in the eternal truths of the gospel. This is as true in encounters with people of other faiths as it is with those whose faith is lapsed or non-existent. Somehow, all these languages must be made comprehensible to each other.

It remains true that mission and evangelism are much more than exercises in propositional knowledge. Words without example are not likely to convince, and it is the example of the Christian community in its ability to mediate God's love through its own corporate life which may be the essential background to evangelism. At the same time, words are still important and often inescapable. Testimony stands alongside practice and the words used must connect with the life in the Christian family. This centrality of the Church – the real, empirical, Church, not just an ideal construct – means that mission always requires ecclesiology. The nature of the community that sends us is key to our identity as missioners.

And yet we live in a culture where words are received, interpreted and disseminated with extraordinary speed – often to the detriment of nuanced understanding. While this points to the importance of the face-to-face dimension in mission and evangelism, where time and trust can enable deep understanding, it also alerts us to the need to be 'media-savvy' and to recognize how our words and actions can be (mis)interpreted by unsympathetic cultures. This is especially important in a social media age where messages and images can so easily be taken out of context and inflame division and ill-feeling.

The Christian Narrative

It is worth looking at how two major contemporary Christian movements, whose work calls us to remember and give attention to the narratives and practices that form the Christian community, understand the way the Church attracts new members.[11] The Radical Orthodoxy movement and Stanley Hauerwas come from very different Christian backgrounds, but both reject the liberal idea that our common humanity, or universal

---

[11] Although we have chosen to use two contemporary theologians to illustrate our point here, many others have also written helpfully on these topics. We would particularly wish to acknowledge the work of Lesslie Newbigin (especially in *The Gospel in a Pluralist Society*, SPCK/Eerdmans, 1989) and John V. Taylor (especially in *The Go-Between God*, SCM, 1972).

understanding of rationality, must be privileged above the specifics of tradition.[12]

For John Milbank, a leading figure in Radical Orthodoxy, the Christian story is, quite simply, the most attractive account of the world and the human condition. Theology is not an adjunct to the social sciences – on the contrary, Christian theology is the prism through which the social sciences make the most sense. The task of Christians is not to persuade others of the truth of the gospel story through propositional argument (which, he claims, always carries undertones of violence) but to 'out narrate' other, rival and less attractive narratives. Christians must so live out their faith in communities that embody the gospel (especially in practices of worship) that others are attracted by the sublime beauty of God reflected in the Church. Conversion, he suggests, is a matter of 'taste' – but in a much more profound sense than that expression is usually used.

Hauerwas's position is similar, although it is arrived at from different starting points. The Church, he argues, is called to be a 'community of character', embodying 'the peaceable kingdom'. It is not called to prop up other social institutions, such as democracy or capitalism, however

---

[12] Milbank is an Anglican who has worked in England and the USA and is currently a professor at Nottingham University. He is prominent in the theological movement known as Radical Orthodoxy, his best-known book being *Theology and Social Theory* (Blackwell, 1991). Hauerwas is, famously, the son of a Texan bricklayer whose Christian identity was formed eclectically in the Southern Methodist and Anabaptist/Mennonite traditions, who taught for many years in a Roman Catholic university and who is now most closely associated with Anglicanism. He is a prolific writer, preacher and essayist.

useful they may be, but to exhibit in its corporate life the radically alternative life of those who follow Christ. Others will wish to join this community, not because they are convinced intellectually of its arguments but because they are captivated by its example of virtuous living.

Both these examples from contemporary theologians are important because they offer a radical missionary ecclesiology. This is an understanding of ecclesiology as the unique vocation of the Church, rather than ecclesiology as the theology of church structures. Similar themes are reflected in the work of many other contemporary theologians, Sam Wells, Stephen Bevans and Graham Tomlin being among the better-known examples.

Most important, perhaps, Milbank, Hauerwas and others make the life of the Church, rather than propositional argument or the techniques of communication, central to the calling of evangelization. In the context of evangelism among people who have their own rich religious culture with its own developed 'language of faith', this may be an important approach to overcoming the immense difficulty of translating between languages of faith. It makes example – the example of the Church as a whole, as well as of individual Christians – the shared vocabulary through which the Christian story may become known.

Trust and the Common Good

While the history of Christian missions sometimes suggests otherwise, it is generally accepted in Britain today that people cannot and indeed should not be coerced into a relationship with Christ. The Great

Commandment alone causes us to draw back from coercive approaches to mission. But if the theological approach noted above is valid, there must be occasions when people of different faiths can encounter each other in sufficient depth for the example of their lives to be knowable. The key to this kind of encounter may lie in the concept of the common good.

To work together for the common good does not, in any way, entail sacrificing the distinctive stories and practices that distinguish the faiths. It is, emphatically, not a reversion to the normlessness that assumes that differences can be subsumed in a single grand narrative.

The pursuit of the common good starts from the observation that we inhabit the same world. In terms of practical politics, the interests of one group or faith are not wholly different from those of another. Examples of such co-working abound, including some of the case studies elsewhere in this report.

Working together for the common good is an end in itself consistent with the Great Commandment, but it is not the only Christian imperative in relating to other faiths. The challenge, as this report will go on to explore, is so to expose ourselves in the process that the very ground of our being – the love of God in Christ – is evident in our lives so that others may encounter Christ and come to faith. So evangelization starts in the holiness and integrity of the lives of Christians, but must then include all manner of communicative actions.

The case studies in this report exemplify this process in action. The guidelines that follow seek to extrapolate from our learning in specific situations so that it can be applied more widely.

> In your hearts set apart Christ as Lord. Always be prepared to give an
> answer to everyone who asks you to give the reason for the hope that
> you have. But do this with gentleness and respect. 1 Peter 15-16 (NIV)

This section seeks to hold together two interconnected strands in
considering the matter of 'good practice'. It offers first, a range of
general reflections drawing on scripture and theology, on the Church's
teaching and on the wide body of experience gained from reflection
on engaging as Christians with individuals and communities of other
faiths. These are from a wide variety of sources with different levels of
authority: some are codes of practice and guidance that may include
formal canonical requirements of the Church of England such as
in relation to worship and the use of consecrated buildings. Others
derive from documents of the Anglican Communion and the Lambeth
Conferences, thereby drawing on the experience of the wider Church.
Others draw on ecumenical and inter faith experience. Some of these
sources of teaching and reflection are given at Appendix 1.

Second, reflections are offered from each of the case studies from
the first edition, drawing from the actual experience of Christians and
the Church in a range of local situations and from the wider experience
of the Church as well as more contemporary models. From these two
strands comes a picture of good practice. It is a general picture that
will need to be worked through in each actual situation in which the
gospel is lived.

In considering the Church's teaching, a distinction may helpfully be
drawn between theology of religions on the one hand and theology of

inter faith relations on the other. Theologies of religions are important in offering a framework for thinking about the relations under God between religions as a whole and are often the unarticulated but formative backdrop to the way in which attitudes are shaped. The Vatican II document Nostra Aetate[1] provided a major impulse for new thinking and reflection on the Christian understanding of other religions in the economy of God.

In 1995 the Doctrine Commission report *The Mystery of Salvation*[2] looked at some of the issues involved here. It suggested that

> there is a plurality of ways by which people are being made whole in the here and now; these are ways the Spirit of God is working. And there is an expectation in the future, that, while people may have the freedom to reject the salvation that is available to all, through God as Trinity, God will save ultimately those who are willing to be saved, by their penitence and acceptance of the love which stretches out to them, in the way that it meets them in their lives and within their traditions. There is only one way, but that way is one that is without barbed wire or boundary fences, so that all may join this way. If we think of salvation in the broadest as encompassing all that heals and enhances human life, then clearly aspects of

---

[1]   www.vatican.va/.../documents/vat-ii_decl_19651028_nostra-aetate_en.html
[2]   The Mystery of Salvation: The Story of God's Gift. A Report by the Doctrine Commission of the Church of England. London: Church House Publishing, 1995, p. 225.

salvation are available in many ways, not only explicitly through Jesus Christ. In the ultimate sense, salvation is defined by having Jesus Christ as its source and goal. To use the terms we deliberately put aside earlier, this pluralism and this exclusivism are reconciled, not in some form of exclusivism (in the usual sense) but eschatologically, in the final purposes of God. To recognize the life, death and resurrection of Jesus as 'constitutive' of salvation as well as revelatory, as Christians do, is to anticipate that he will prove to be the definitive focus of salvation in its fully comprehensive form. It may be, too, that our understanding of Christ will itself be enhanced when people of other faiths are gathered in.[3]

The report further declares that although we restrict the fullness of God's love if we deny 'the truth and goodness which Christ as Logos, and God by the Spirit, can also inspire in those of other faiths and of none', nevertheless Christians believe

that God has chosen to provide the fullest revelation of his love for all humanity in the cross and resurrection. Hence we naturally pray that God will bring all people, including those of other faiths, to explicit faith in Christ and membership of his Church. This is not because we believe that the God revealed in Christ is unable to save them without this, but because Christ is the truest and fullest expression of his love, and we long for them to share it. In the Lord's words in St John's Gospel, 'I came that they might have life, and have it abundantly.'[4]

---

[3] *The Mystery of Salvation*, pp. 183–4.
[4] *The Mystery of Salvation*, p. 184.

The approach taken in the Doctrine Commission's report explains why the Church of England can seek simultaneously to develop good relations with people of other faiths, to work constructively with them in projects that promote the common good and at the same time be committed, in obedience to the great commission, to enabling all people, including those of other religions, to come to faith in Jesus Christ, to baptism and to full participation in the life of the Church.

A theology of inter faith relations speaks into the situation of actual engagement between human beings, particularly with other faiths than Christian. It discourages prior assumptions about the other and encourages consideration of the gospel bases for engagement. Particular mention may be made here of the document *Generous Love – an Anglican Theology of Inter Faith Relations*, discussed at the 2008 Lambeth Conference[5] and commended by General Synod in 2009. This offers a theology of interreligious relations that is shaped by the contours of the fundamental Christian doctrine of God as Trinity.

Generous Love speaks helpfully of 'embassy' and 'hospitality' as two 'heart' movements of the mission of God: embassy, as the necessary consequence of the outward moving nature of the love of God expressed most fully in the life, death and resurrection of Jesus and in the work of the Holy Spirit; and hospitality as the welcome and openness that is at the heart of the God who is love. Both these movements should be

---

[5] *Generous Love: The truth of the Gospel and the call to dialogue. An Anglican theology of inter faith relations*. A report from the Anglican Communion Network for Inter Faith Concerns. Published by the Anglican Consultative Council 2008.

observable in the life of Christian communities as they relate to those among whom they live, not as means to an end, but as a natural outworking of lives oriented to the gospel.

A rootedness in scripture and in an understanding of its originating contexts provides a foundation for good practice in sharing the gospel. A Church that has generally been unused to reading and studying the Bible with its multi religious context in mind will find much to wrestle with and to be encouraged by. A note of caution is in order, that as in biblical interpretation in general, it is important to avoid taking individual texts out of their wider context. There can be a temptation to apply particular texts to current inter religious settings inappropriately.

Both Testaments offer a challenging range of encounters between the people of God and people and communities of other religions. Sometimes the encounters appear aggressively and violently hostile as in the accounts of Elijah and the prophets of Baal; sometimes there are deeply moving stories involving human relationships across religious divides, as in Ruth; other stories illustrate the profound challenge to existing ways of thinking as in the encounter of Jesus with the Syro-Phoenician woman. Perhaps above all the stories of mould-breaking encounters with Samaritans[6] – the Samaritan village and Samaritan

---

[6] Matthew 10.5; John 4.9; Luke 10.25; Luke 17.10; John 4.6; Acts 8.25.

woman at the well of Jacob[7] for example – provide much apposite reflection for our present society.

From these and many other sources of teaching and reflection it may be said that what is good practice will be rooted in a profound reflection on and appreciation of the *Missio Dei* – the outward movement of the God who is love towards the creation that is the focus of that love. From this understanding of the nature of love and truth in Trinitarian relationship comes an approach to mission that gives the Church a central role but one that is subordinate to the overarching and prior mission of God.

It is an approach that gladly acknowledges that the Holy Spirit is at work in the world and that its fruits are seen in lives of love, joy and peace. It holds together in creative tension both hospitality and embassy – the roles of host and guest. It proclaims gladly and openly the uniqueness of the work of God in the life, death, resurrection and ascension of Jesus Christ and for that reason it gives extreme value to each human being in their own right. It forbears from making ultimate judgements about others, always preferring to leave that to the loving mercy of Christ.

In this approach, sharing the gospel of salvation through Christ alone is not an exercise in the selling of a product in a competitive marketplace of religions or philosophies, it is proclamation. In response

---

[7] At the end of the passage her compatriots proclaim Jesus 'Saviour of the World'. This is the one occasion in the New Testament where this expression is used. It is of interest therefore that this is as the result of a dialogue between two people that this confession is made and provides a model for evangelism.

to a question[8] on this in 2009, the then Archbishop of Canterbury, Rowan Williams, responded:

> Evangelism in the New Testament is first of all, proclamation. 'This has happened. This is the door that is open. Walk in and welcome.' And that is what I believe the Church should be saying every hour. 'Come in. It'll challenge you and change you and it won't be easy; but you can live with that!' Evangelism then becomes primarily saying to people, 'There are more possibilities for you than you could ever have imagined, thanks to the grace and mercy of God and Jesus Christ'. Now, I think that's a bit different from saying, 'This is the best product in the market and unless you buy it your friends won't want to know you', (which I caricature as a sort of marketing strategy). I believe that the Christian faith is true. I believe that the God it speaks about is the real, living God. And I believe that the highest and fullest possibilities of human beings are realized in Christ-like relationship through the Holy Spirit with that one, true, living God our Father. That's axiomatic for me. And that doesn't mean that I want to say at the same time, 'Outside that, everything is darkness, failure and hopelessness.' It means I know what God has shown himself to be in Jesus Christ; I want others to see that, to share it and live in it and with it. Exactly how God relates to those who don't see their way in, is God's business. And that for me is not at all incompatible with wanting to say to my Muslim, or Hindu or Buddhist friends, 'I wish you could see things like this.'

---

[8] At a seminar in June 2009 by the Contextual Theology Centre at The Royal Foundation of St Katharine.

Meanwhile, in that encounter, when they are saying the same thing back to me, I hope I'm growing a little bit in response to that challenge. Where you can say, 'Yes, when the Muslim says that, that's not stupid or trivial. I hadn't thought of that' or when the Buddhist says, 'Life is like this' and you think, 'Well, maybe the way I've assimilated Christianity has left that out. I need to hear that', that's the joy of inter faith encounter which sends me back to my starting point: I still believe that door is open, and that's what I proclaim and offer.

Now, I think the practical difficulty in deeply plural communities these days of separating that glad invitation from what's felt to be bullying or manipulative or threatening is not straightforward – because we have a history (as also do other religions) of being bullying and manipulative. We've all fallen short of the glory of whatever God we turn to, and that'll always cloud people's perception of one another. So it's a hard line to tread; but I don't think it's impossible.

In this way of understanding there is no conflict between 'dialogue' and 'evangelism' since both are part of proclamation. These are not 'either/or' but 'both/and', held together as our response to the mission of God in Christ. Dialogue may sometimes mistakenly be seen as something completely separated from evangelism; it may also be given a mistakenly restricted meaning and role. To speak of dialogue is not just to refer an esoteric activity undertaken by experts or enthusiasts. It is to speak of the many ways in which human beings relate to each other particularly across religious or other differences.

Much has been written about dialogue and many guidelines helpfully offered. Some of these are given in Appendix 3. The commonly used fourfold classification of dialogue is helpful: the dialogue of daily life – encounters on the doorstep or at the checkout; the dialogue of the common good – engagement together in tasks beneficial to the community; the dialogue of mutual understanding – often in more formalized structures or conversations such as Scriptural Reasoning,[9] and the dialogue of spiritual life – encountering each other at prayer and worship.

There are of course very many situations and contexts in which Christians share the gospel of salvation with others. Any selection of particular cases raises questions about what it means to share the gospel, about understandings of salvation, about criteria to be used in discerning good practice and about the selection of one particular set of case studies rather than others.

The simple testimony of the spoken word describing personal experience will always be a part of the Christian life, but fully to share the gospel of salvation is to live a life that offers to others the possibility of choosing to be a disciple of Christ as Lord and Saviour. This requires some combination of word and deed. Such a life, lived individually or collectively, may have as a conscious intent the sharing of the gospel story with others; or the life may simply be lived in Christ and in so doing may be so attractive that it raises questions among those who observe it and are affected by it. There is a continuum from living as an explicit and overt witness, to a life that is known to God alone.

---

[9] At a seminar in June 2009 by the Contextual Theology Centre at The Royal Foundation of St Katharine.

Nevertheless, to say as above that evangelism and dialogue are held together in proclamation, is not to say that there are no distinctions between them, and it is important to address specific issues in relation to evangelism[10] in multi faith contexts. What follows is a reflection on evangelism from a multi religious parish context:

> We are aware in our parish that evangelism is a sensitive issue not least because the majority of people who live in our area hold to a different faith. Some of these people may not like us wanting to share our faith with them, for a variety of different reasons. This is a particular issue with Jewish people because of the Church's painful history of anti-Semitism and the deep concern of some Jews about so many young people 'marrying out'. But also Hindus, Sikhs and Jains find the thought of conversion very difficult, and this has been a painful issue over the last few years especially in Hindu Christian relations. We know too that the consequences of evangelism for some converts, especially from different faiths to Christianity, could be great hurt to their families and themselves and could even lead to danger. There is the historical heritage of which we are reminded where Christians, particularly in colonial contexts, have used positions of power to exert unethical pressure on people of different faiths to convert to Christianity. There is also a feeling by some both

---

[10] Christian discourse uses a range of words to speak of the activity of presenting the gospel: evangelism, mission, witness, proclamation, proselytism. Care needs to be taken in the use of the different terminology each of which carry different meaning and implication. Increasingly, 'proselytizing' has been used with negative connotation to imply the use of inappropriate methods.

outside of and inside the Church that evangelism will inevitably create conflict and possibly even violence, and so should be avoided.

Nevertheless, Christians in our congregation still pray for and desire to share their faith with others, of all religious backgrounds. The foremost reasons stated probably among our congregation would be that Christians are called to do this in the Bible, and that there is a natural desire on the part of Christians to want to share the good news that they have found in Christ with others. It is important also to us that we have fellow Christians among us who have come to Christ from a variety of different religious backgrounds, and these people are clear that what they have found is a good thing and they are grateful that someone shared Christ with them, even if their road has been difficult. There is also a sense among some of us that our whole society and particularly our political and educational systems are based on the assumption that people have a right to persuade others and to be persuaded by others in a whole variety of disciplines from science to politics. If a politician can show up on my doorstep to persuade me to vote for her and not the candidate I have voted for in the past, or a television programme can try to persuade me to accept a position for (or against) global warming, why can't a person try to persuade someone else to embrace a faith or a different faith? We know Muslims, Buddhists, Hindus and Humanists who share their faith (or lack of it) with us, and who have 'converts' within their respective communities so that faith sharing and conversion is for many simply part of the experience of living in a multi faith society.

The real issue for us as a congregation, however, is not whether we should engage in evangelism, but rather how we should do that, and in particular how we can do it ethically. In this area we are grateful for the work done by the Christian Muslim Forum, established under the patronage of the Archbishop of Canterbury, in taking forward an initiative of the Youth Encounter Programme of Scripture Union known as 'Ethical Guidelines for Christian and Muslim Witness in Britain'. Although these guidelines have been developed in the context of Christian Muslim relations, they offer help and encouragement in the wider context of faith sharing between members of different faiths.[11]

Part of our experience of being a minority community as Christians in our particular context is an increased confidence that if our motivation is genuinely loving, and we are careful to be ethical in the way we evangelize, we don't need to be apologetic about sharing who we are and what we have discovered in Christ. Our religious context increasingly feels like a 'level playing field' with the different faith communities rooted and confident in themselves and a clearer sense that we can all relate to each other as co-citizens rather than as 'hosts' or 'guests'.

Our experience is that Churches of all denominations in multi faith areas often engage in evangelistic activities similar to those in other non-religious contexts, neither 'targeting' people of other faiths, nor excluding them either. So, for example, many churches offer the Alpha Course to which, from time to time, people of different faiths

---

[11] Appendix 3 and at www.christianmuslimforum.org/downloads/Ethical_Guidelines_for_Witness.pdf

will come, and some of those will over time become Christians. Congregations in multi faith areas will often participate in a wider 'mission' event and invite their friends and neighbours to come along. Our experience is that these invitations are often warmly received, with maybe a comment such as, "We're glad that the Church is doing something to show people a different way than the immoral and self-destructive ways that we see them living." Congregation members will be encouraged to invite their neighbours to special services such as 'Back to Church Sunday' and we find that in a multi faith area some of these people who come will be from different faith backgrounds. Mostly people will hear about the Christian faith simply through a friendship, but for others it may be through a specific initiative of the church such as the distribution of DVDs of the 'Jesus' film, or teams of congregation members visiting homes to offer to pray for specific needs. Many clergy in multi faith areas have had the experience of being approached by people of a different faith for some kind of deliverance ministry, and when this is provided it sometimes leads to the person embracing the Christian faith.

Our multi faith society is in a constant process of change, and there are many from different faith backgrounds who are more prepared than before to move outside of the faith communities into which they have grown up. While not necessarily wanting to 'sign up' as Christians, there are those who are deeply drawn to the person of Christ as they find him in and through the Christian community, or directly through dreams and healings. Our churches have found that we need to let people come at their own speed and in their own ways, and not try to rush a decision that they are not yet ready to make. Our experience is that those who come into the church fellowship from different faith backgrounds often have a long and difficult journey. Some of those who come into the church come from the 'edges' of their own communities, and many do not have the same sense of loyalty to a particular congregation as we see in those who have grown up in the church or who come from a nominal Christian background.

In relation to people and communities of other faiths, there are many ministries that seek consciously to offer the gospel story in ways that are specifically designed to speak appropriately to Muslims, Jews or Hindus for example. Various ministries to and among people of other religions seek to understand those religions and to offer the gospel story to them in terms that connect with their narratives and cultural contexts. There are also courses and programmes that seek to equip Christians to understand their own faith more deeply with the intent that they will be better equipped for the contexts in which they will encounter people and communities of other faiths, particularly where these also have their equivalent of approaches to mission.

Other gospel ministries are committed to the provision of particular services of care to the homeless, to broken families, to children and youth, to the sick or to any number of communities of need. These are driven by a desire to share the gospel of salvation through practical witness to the love of God for all people as expressed in the healing and reconciling ministry of Christ. Such ministries may be intentionally located in particular social environments or may simply grow from a life lived and the religious composition of the people ministered to will vary according to the locality.

Chaplaincy is a particular form of Christian ministry which has developed over many centuries and is widely recognized and appreciated. Chaplaincy is essentially a pastoral ministry, offering the gospel of salvation through the pastoral, prayer and liturgical ministry of countless Christians, stipendiary and voluntary. This may be in public institutions such as hospitals and hospices, prisons, the armed forces, higher and further education institutions; but also across the whole range of society, in industry, schools and sport and in a myriad of other contexts where people are gathered for particular reasons and purposes. Where chaplaincy ministry is offered through public sector institutions, the National Health Service for example, it is increasingly offered alongside and in collaboration with chaplains of other faiths than Christian. Christian chaplaincy in the public sector seeks to maintain a distinctive Christian witness while respecting the norms of the public-sector institutions.

The teaching ministry of Christians who specialize in the scholarly and academic work of understanding other religions and making that understanding available to others to assist them in their ministry is of great importance. This is a form of witness that is undertaken within theological colleges and courses, within academic contexts with a Christian framework and other academic institutions of a secular nature within the norms of the Academy. The Centre for Muslim-Christian Studies in Oxford,[12] and in previous years the London School of Theology's Centre for Islamic Studies, and the Heythrop College Centre for Christianity and Interreligious Dialogue provide examples of such

----

[12] www.cmcsoxford.org.uk

institutions but there are many other such ministries. These include the work of the *Building Bridges Seminar* of Christian and Muslim scholars and others involved in a very wide range of study and publication. The Christian-Muslim Forum arranges seminars and discussions between scholars of both traditions.

A further major context within which the gospel of salvation is offered and from which examples of good practice may be drawn, is that of primary and secondary education through nearly 5,000 church schools – and by individual teachers in other maintained sector schools. The Church of England and other Christian Churches provide education within a Christian framework to millions of children and young people in maintained sector neighbourhood schools across the country. The religious composition of the neighbourhoods in which schools are located varies widely, but in many areas now include significant communities of other faiths than Christian. In such contexts the pupils at a school may be religiously mixed or in some cases may be substantially of one non-Christian religion. Christian ministry in schools respects the religious belonging of all pupils but offers a context within which Christian faith is lived and taught empathetically and openly. It is for these reasons that so many families of other faiths than Christian are content for their children to attend Church schools.[13]

---

[13] The General Synod debated the Church of England Schools' Strategy in February 2007. The document 'Achieving the First Two Hundred Years' reviews achievements against the recommendations of the Dearing Commission, *The Way Ahead* published in 2001 and develops the strategy for the period up to the bi-Centenary of the National Society in 2011.

There has in recent years been a growth in the number and scope of structured multi religious Forums and Councils, with varying sustainability and success,[14] very often initiated and sustained by Christians. These have come together for the purposes of greater mutual understanding and for common action for the benefit of society. While many motives may be involved in their development, including the support of government cohesion and other policies, at the heart of Christian engagement is a desire to know the other and to be known truthfully and empathetically by the other. This is an important means by which Christians and people of other faiths witness to each other in the integrity of their self-understandings. The situations in which such Forums and Councils have grown up and the ways in which they operate are multifarious and in some cases longstanding, with the Council of Christians and Jews having been founded in 1942.[15] Others, like the Inter Faith Network for the UK and the Christian-Muslim Forum,[16] are further examples of national structures, although there are also many regional and more local forums and Councils as well.

In addition to these specific ministries and usually inter-related with them, is the life of the local parish church in all its varied expressions which is the bedrock of the Church of England. It is in and through the collective life of worship and service to the people of the parish that the

---

[14]   The Inter Faith Network for the UK mentions 25 national, 14 regional and 217 local inter faith bodies in its 2007 Directory of Inter Faith Organizations in the UK.

[15]   www.ccj.org.uk/.

[16]   www.christianmuslimforum.org/.

gospel of salvation through Christ alone is most widely lived out and offered to people of all faiths and none in the ordinary circumstances of their daily lives. It is from this context that the case studies that follow have been mainly chosen on the basis that it is in this context that most people encounter the lived life of Christian communities and from which very many of the specific ministries are grown and nurtured.

The charge given to the minister of a parish is that of the 'cure of souls', a responsibility for the care and cure (healing) of what is essential to the wellbeing of human beings.[17] This traditional phrase provides a very positive present day means of understanding what the offering of the gospel of salvation involves in the context of parishes with the widest variety of parishioners of all faiths and none.

There are some 13,000 Church of England parishes across the country each offering its way of living out the gospel story of salvation through Christ among its wider parish community.

> Over 1,000 of these parish churches live their lives among parish populations in which more than 10% of people are of other faiths, accounting in total for over one quarter of the total population of England.

---

[17] 'The word "cure" has two overtones. It means "care", and it means "cure" in the sense of "healing". When we use the phrase, we are saying that the church has responsibility to care for those in the community, but also has responsibility for bringing healing into people's souls. It must work to enable their souls to be healthy.' The Rt Revd Brian Smith, June 2009.

The *Presence and Engagement* programme initiated by General Synod in 2005 seeks to support and equip these parishes and to enable a sharing of the wide variety of ways in which they live out and share the gospel.[18] When the mandate for the Presence and Engagement programme was renewed at the General Synod of July 2017, a core stated vision for the next quinquennium was 'that churches become confident in sharing the gospel sensitively and effectively with people from other backgrounds, and welcoming those who embrace Christian faith'.[19]

The case studies that follow are drawn from the contexts of these parish churches and therefore have a particular focus on mission in significant communities of people of other faiths. Six are given, drawn from a countless number that could have been provided. A further ten are mentioned in Appendix 3 to provide a glimpse of the wider backdrop from which they are drawn. The Presence and Engagement website at www.presenceandengagement.org.uk has been developed to gather the widest range of ways in which the gospel is lived out and offered among people of all faiths and none, and additional resources can be found there.

---

[18] GS 1577. *Presence and Engagement – the churches' task in a multi faith society.* Report by the Mission and Public Affairs Council, July 2005.
[19] http://presenceandengagement.org.uk/sites/default/files/Report%20to%20 General%20Synod%20July%202017.pdf p. 5 (accessed 13.12.2018).

6 Examples and Commendations of Good Practice in Sharing the Gospel of Salvation Through Christ Alone with People of Other Faiths and of None

In considering the following 2010 snapshots, it will be important to hold in mind the general assumptions about good practice sketched above; that these are a small sample from only one arena in which the gospel is shared with others; and that these are summary descriptions of situations involving many people over long periods.

The examples summarized below – in which the local church tells its own story – are drawn from the dioceses of Leicester (St Philip's), London (Southall), Birmingham (Springfield), St Albans (All Saints, Bedford), Blackburn (Building Bridges in Burnley) and Bradford (St Clement and St Augustine) and to that extent seek to encompass a wide geographic range and a variety of different contexts.

From Leicester, the example of a church striking out in a radically new direction to offer its experience as an asset for the wider Church. From Southall comes an example of the way in which the gospel is shared through common action for the improvement of the local environment. From Birmingham, an illustration of the ways in which a local church's involvement with the families and children of its parish has led to a major public investment. From Bedford, the work of a parish church through story, song and sport. From Burnley, the engagement of churches with other faith communities for understanding and reconciliation; and from Bradford an example of the life of a church in one of the most multi religious contexts in the country.

St Philip's Centre, Leicester

Leicester developed as a city with significant communities of other faiths primarily from the early 1970s with the expulsion of Asians from Uganda under General Idi Amin. From that time substantial Hindu and Sikh and also Muslim communities have grown, including latterly a significant Somali population. Estimates are that Hindus and Muslims are about equal in number, and there is a significant move of more prosperous South Asians to suburban and rural Leicestershire.

St Philip's parish has been among many parishes that have changed dramatically in recent decades. From being a substantial congregation drawing on a parish population of Christian culture, the church has moved to being a small congregation in a parish with one of the smallest Christian percentage population in the UK and set in the midst of Muslim, Hindu and Sikh people. The church building is now opposite a substantial newly-built mosque across the road, a miniature version of one of the great domed mosques in Istanbul, with several hundred attending each day, and with no places available on Fridays or during Ramadan.

Two crucial decisions were made in relationship to the church. A major fire in 1996 led to debate as to whether to remain open, in view of the changing demography around. The Bishop of the time took the decision that for this very reason they should remain open as a living witness, and a major refurbishment took place, to allow for community use. The second decision was made in 2005 to remain present and to engage with this changed context in a strikingly new way and the St Philip's Centre has developed from this decision.

The Parochial Church Council decided to enter into a partnership with the Diocese of Leicester and the national Presence and Engagement programme to become a means through which the experience of living out the gospel in the midst of people of other faiths could be offered to other churches locally and regionally. To this end it invested part of its financial reserves, its vicarage, its church buildings and its lived life in the creation and sustaining of the St Philip's Centre.

St Philip's Centre is rooted in the multi faith context of Leicester and is a national ecumenical training centre under the Presence and Engagement initiative. It provides training for Christians, for those of other faiths and for civic partners. It enables Christians and churches to be a confident presence in a multi faith world, prepared to share their own faith and learn from others. Good working relationships and dialogue with peoples of other faiths serve to promote the common good. The emphasis is to include those who live, work and minister in suburbs, small towns and villages, who are all, in various ways and with various challenges, part of a multi faith society.

What might be learnt from this experience which can be shared with others?
* That continuous physical presence in a community whose nature is radically changing provides the basis for deep engagement with incoming people of other faiths.

- That a shared and mutually supportive relationship between the local church, the diocese and other Christian denominations brings benefits of resources, encouragement and common purpose.
- Core support from the Bishop, the Bishop's Council and the Diocesan Synod, has been vital, and generous, as the Centre is seen as a Centre for mission.
- That an explicitly Christian community can be appreciated, respected and used by other Faith communities and by secular authorities in a wide range of programmes for the common good.
- That a strong local centre can contribute greatly to the international, national and regional Church and beyond, through the wide use of its staff, several of whom have an academic reputation, and especially are known for their link of the academic with the practical.
- That multi faith relations are about relations also with particular faith communities. Leicester and the Centre provide an ideal base for engaging with the Hindu traditions of the largely Indian diaspora, in balance with Islam and Judaism.
- That a Centre can be deeply rooted in Christ, and in Christian scripture, clear about the saving grace of God offered in Christ, but at the same time, be deeply committed to the message that 'There's a wideness in God's mercy ...'

A Rocha, Southall

Southall is a community with one of the most diverse religious populations in England and with a particularly large Sikh community and one of the largest gurdwaras in the country immediately opposite the church of St John the Evangelist, Southall Green. It includes over 50 separate places of worship, among which are six Church of England parish churches, all with congregations of great ethnic diversity. The diversity of the congregations of Southall speaks strongly to the universality of the gospel.

A Rocha UK is part of the international A Rocha movement, a family of projects and initiatives running practical environmental projects in 18 countries across six continents. It is a Christian organization, working to show God's love for the whole creation and to take the creation care message to those that need to hear it. A Rocha's vision is 'the transformation of people and places, as individuals and communities do their bit to care for God's world'. A Rocha UK has now grown into one of the UK's leading Christian environmental charities, with several projects around the country, and partnerships with several major Christian bodies.

A Rocha UK began its life in Southall. The initiatives in Southall played an important part in transforming the local environment of Southall, beginning simply with the placing of recycling banks on local church premises and developing into a concern about high levels of air pollution and large amounts of litter in public places. Southall also had the lowest ratio of public green space per household in England with an accompanying increased likelihood of mental health difficulties among those deprived of access to green spaces.

What might be learnt from this experience which can be shared with others?

- That a concern for the stewardship of the local environment goes hand in hand with a concern for the physical, mental and spiritual wellbeing of those who live in it.
- That explicit Christian concern and action can be a powerful source of energy to bring together people of all faith and none.
- That small and local initiatives can grow to have national impact.
- That the relationships and shared values of care for creation also provide an opportunity for Christian witness and sharing of faith.

St Christopher's, Springfield Children's Centre, Birmingham

The Diocese of Birmingham, after the Diocese of London, had the highest proportion of parishes at the 2011 census, with more than 10% of people of other faiths, and this will have grown significantly since then. Although the main faiths are all present across Birmingham, many Presence and Engagement parishes in the south and east of the city have predominantly Muslim communities, with others in the northern and western areas having in addition significant Hindu and Sikh communities.

The neighbourhoods of Saltley, Bordesley, Small Heath, Sparkbrook, Sparkhill and Springfield include between them the largest Muslim community in the country. The life and witness of the churches and Christian communities in these neighbourhoods must take this fully into account if the gospel of salvation is to be attractive and attracting. St Christopher's, Springfield is an inner-city parish with a majority Muslim community but also with smaller Hindu and Sikh communities. In serving these and families of no faith in the area, key points in the Church's calendar and in the rhythms of the project have provided opportunities for creative expressions of the Christian story. 'In appropriately ethical ways, the Church has been exploring ways of learning from South Asian spiritualities in a Christ-centred journey that facilitates connections with our community and honours the search for God that is so real for many in our context.'

Again, those involved tell the story in their own words:

'Over recent years, a vital relationship of dialogue has developed with the large mosque facing the Church. The very nature of our environment and the problem of religious extremism globally give us a keen sense that we should foster a spirituality that is faithful to our texts and tradition and equally committed to be a blessing to all in our city, whatever their faith. The congregation consists of old and young, white, black, South Asian, professional and non-professional and believes that diversity within the Church is part of the gospel we offer to the world.'

The Springfield Project is a community project established in 2000 by St Christopher's church and the Springfield Children's Centre and is a completely new facility for childcare.

Birmingham City Council chose the existing 'Seedlings' project, a multi faith playschool run by St Christopher's church, as the basis for an investment of over £2 million and to create one of the City's Children's Centres. The Springfield Project began when a few mothers within the congregation started a play school but when only two or three families attended for the first year they came close to giving up. However, in the second year, 'Seedlings' began to flourish. One key aspect of the earliest phase was that the people involved had some professional training as nursery workers and put much work into developing a structured programme of games and learning activities. It was the quality of the environment, the play-materials and the attention of the carers that made it grow in popularity. From the beginning, Bible studies that resonated with the Muslim faith were read in story time and prayer was offered and accepted.

What might be learnt from this experience which can be shared with others?

- That when a consistent commitment is shown by the people of a church to all the people of a parish whatever their faith, then the secular authorities may be willing to invest public funds and to accept the continuing witness of the Church.
- That being a minority within a Muslim majority neighbourhood does not inhibit a Christian community from being outward looking, confident and inspirational.

- That engaging on equal terms with people of other faiths does not compromise Christian faith and witness to the gospel of salvation through Christ alone.

Bedford: All Saints, Diocese of St Albans

The Diocese of St Albans had some 35 out of 335 parishes with more than 10% of their populations of other faiths at the 2001 census. The parishes include some 20% of the diocesan population. All Saints, Bedford in the Queen's Park area has a significant Muslim community as well as smaller Hindu and Sikh communities. Put simply, All Saints Parish Church fosters friendships across religious lines. The church runs several community projects with strong though often understated inter faith components. Church members work closely with the leaders of the nearby mosque and gurdwara and have developed a Faith Tour that brings thousands of school children to the three places of worship each year.

Fusion Youth Singing was a project using music to foster social cohesion. In 2008 the group turned to drama and presented a musical called *Jigsaw* that enabled young people to engage with the stories of those from very different backgrounds.

As a parish church, All Saints has developed a number of initiatives that seek to witness to the love of God in Christ for all and that engage with the lives of parishioners of all faiths and none, young and old.

All Saints Basketball Club was started by eight teenage church members in 2003. A year later it had grown to include 80 children. The players and volunteer coaches reflect the religious and cultural diversity of the neighbourhood. Nearly half the players are girls who may train and play with the boys but who also have their own teams. Players improve their sporting ability but the emphasis is on their emotional, social and spiritual development.

For the then deputy churchwarden Neslyn Pearson, inter religious encounter affords opportunities to both proclaim and deepen her faith: 'Whether coaching a girls' team on the cricket pitch or conversing with Muslims over a plate of samosas about our self-surrender to God, I'm often called to re-think my faith and to articulate it in new ways. Being a Christian in a multi faith parish is a wonderful vocation.'

What might be learnt from these experiences which can be shared with others?

- That a local parish church can engage creatively with the stories of parishioners from all faiths and none in ways that open doors to trusting relationships which are a witness to the gospel.
- That music and song can be a means to bring young people, including young Muslim people, together provided that cultural norms are respected.
- That living out the Church of England's self understanding of having the cure of souls is capable of effective re-articulation in a multi religious environment.

Building Bridges, Burnley

In 2001 there were serious disturbances in Burnley and in other northern towns and cities involving young people from different communities. Since then the whole community has worked together to increase understanding between different ethnic groups and a number of initiatives have resulted involving mainly local churches and mosques. One central initiative has been *Building Bridges Burnley,* which was founded in the year following the riots. BBB is based in the Masjid-e-Ibrahim Mosque and involves almost all the Christian clergy in the borough as well as all the Imams. They have run regular inter faith events, including shared meals, involving over 400 people, hosted by local churches and mosques alternately, discussion forums and a range of women-only seminars. Some of these discussions have addressed difficult issues such as issues for Christians in Pakistan around blasphemy laws and the challenge of conversion across faiths.

One of the considerable innovations has been the development of pilgrimages, which regularly involve some 15–20 people, both Christians and Muslims, men and women. These pilgrimages have been to such places as London, Rome and Jerusalem. The experience widely shared with others in Burnley has led to a deepening understanding and trust between the faith communities.

What might be learnt from this experience which can be shared with others?

● The key need is to develop trust between what were once separate communities; the separation being on faith, race and cultural lines. The local Presence and Engagement churches have been committed to this reconciliation.

- That in situations of tension, churches, other faith communities and local authorities working together can ease the possibility of conflict.
- Being nice to one another is not enough. Hard questions have to be faced once trust is established.
- An awareness that we are in for the long haul and this is more important than quick results.
- Commitment to inter faith dialogues requires a readiness to be honest, open to challenge and public scrutiny.
- That Christians and churches working together ecumenically are a stronger witness to the gospel than being perceived as separated or discordant.

St Augustine and St Clement, Bradford

The congregations of the parishes of St Augustine and St Clement in the Barkerend and Undercliffe neighbourhoods of east Bradford live their Christian lives in a context in which nearly three quarters of their parishioners are Muslim. They offer an experience of gospel proclamation from which the wider Church can learn.

From the Gospel according to St Mark 4.26: 'Jesus also said, "This is what the kingdom of God is like. A man scatters seed on the ground. Night and day, whether he sleeps or gets up, the seed sprouts and grows, though he does not know how. All by itself the soil produces grain – first the stalk, then the head, then the full kernel in the head. As soon as the grain is ripe, he puts the sickle to it, because the harvest has come."'

It is clear that this kingdom is not one that provides simple answers. We live in one of the most Muslim contexts in the UK. In addition there is the main Hindu temple, and five of the six Sikh gurdwaras of the city are in our neighbourhood.

It is normal for people of other faiths to walk into both of our buildings because of our social action which is freely offered, no strings attached – indeed one of our buildings houses a municipal library. One mother who came in said that she had never felt closer to God than in our building as a child. Will she become a Christian? It is not for us to ask. There is too much at stake for her. But she will influence her children. Possibly another member of her family may come to faith and pave the way for her.

Our social action includes caring for mainly white Christian elders, offering a toddler group, teaching gardening, showing people how to plant tubs and baskets for their yards. These actions, and a community centre in which the church was a founding partner, are one of the few places in our area of the city where people meet across race, faith and cultural boundaries.

There have been a number of visits to places of worship of the other faith communities locally. When a large new mosque was built close to one of our churches, and right in our view of the centre of our city, we arranged a visit. The parish priest was invited to the opening and took a guest from the church who lived very close. We welcomed the world leader of this sect of Islam to our city in the name of Jesus Christ. Either we could see this community as an intrusion, or as neighbours for whom Christ died. The follow up visit was for many in the churches their first visit to a mosque. We were very well received. Yes, we are aware of the evangelical intent of this group. But they have reciprocated our visits, and there is a genuine dialogue and mutual listening.

What might be learnt from this experience which can be shared with others?

- The cross and the resurrection of Christ, as always, are subversive of political and religious authority. Facile answers to questions about mission, race, faith, culture and power will not do. It does not matter whether these questions come from the local authority, other faith communities or from within the Christian faith.
- The continued Christian presence in the inner city is subversive too for any who think of it as their space and for some who think of it as not their space.
- Stories of mission that include the realities of sharing something of the sufferings of Christ on the cross are a part of our Christian witness.

Concluding Reflections

The phrase 'to share the gospel of salvation in Christ alone' may be considered by some confrontational and incompatible with current cultural understandings of freedom, inclusiveness, cohesion and choice. It will also and sadly sometimes be misunderstood as provocative or even hostile. How the gospel is shared and how it is received will depend on the extent to which examples of the kind illustrated above are taken to heart. The challenge is to show clearly that our intention is to express the overflowing love of God, Father, Son and Holy Spirit, for all human beings as expressed in the life, death on the cross and resurrection of Jesus Christ, freely offered to all.

These snapshots of engagement with other faiths can be repeated in similar ways throughout England. Many of these illustrations have deepened their involvement, extending project work, drawing from fresh funding sources, and launching fresh initiatives. St John's Southall, for example, is now embarking on a new phase in the development of the proposed 'King's Centre'. It aims to be a base resourcing mission and ministry in the heart of multi religious Southall, with a clear mandate to equip church planting in areas of religious diversity. It is sobering to note, however, that since 2010, some of these church projects have closed down due to lack of funding or personnel.

St Christopher's Springfield remains a key hub for Children's Centre activity now for the whole city of Birmingham with additional ministries within its Springfield Project arm that seek to provide housing. There is also an Asian fellowship within the congregation and a staff member who is a convert from Sikhism who heads up this work.

What is evident when the gospel of salvation is shared across cultural and religious divides is that church communities will inevitably change. Patterns of worship and discipleship need to change to reflect the cultural contexts of converts, and those in leadership will increasingly need to be drawn from those backgrounds. How the Church of England plans ahead, with vision, for urban and inner city contexts of especial religious diversity is an imminent challenge. The benchmark of 10% of other faiths to be a designated Presence and Engagement parish is becoming a normative reality for so much of the Church of England. To continue to draw on these stories of being a transformative and transformed presence in those areas we most associate with religious diversity is a gift to the present and future of the whole Church of England.

One significant development since the original publication of *Sharing the Gospel of Salvation* in 2010 has been the growth in numbers of converts among the Persian diaspora. Large numbers of Iranians from a Muslim background have become Christians, finding themselves in clusters of communities in a number of urban parishes across England. The extent of these numbers and their cultural needs in the process of catechesis have meant that in March 2019 a Persian-language Church of England eucharistic liturgy was launched at Wakefield Cathedral.

There are already a number of Church of England priests from Muslim, Sikh and Hindu backgrounds, and these numbers are growing. As we share the gospel of salvation, attention to the need for ordained and lay leadership to reflect the changing nature of the Church will become ever greater.

What additional reflections about good practice can be drawn from these few examples, beyond those from existing documents and publications? Although this document has given particular attention to contexts in which people and communities of other faiths are significantly present, nevertheless good practice in sharing the gospel has the same characteristics in all contexts and so these reflections are relevant more widely.

Christianity takes the facts of human existence and the context within which human lives are lived very seriously. The incarnation: the coming-among-us of Jesus Christ, his life, death in the raw situations of human communities and their politics, his relationships of challenging love with those around him from high to low and with fellow Jews and pagan Romans, his continuing resurrected encounter with people today – all these provide the rationale for taking these things seriously in our own times and places.

Sharing the gospel is always done in the context of the lives of other people who are created in the image of God. There is always a context of place and time, of relationship, of history and of mutual knowledge or ignorance. Without a whole-hearted attempt to enter into such contexts, the risks of the gospel being misunderstood, unappreciated or rejected outright are greatly increased. 'Guarding the treasure that has been entrusted to us' is not a responsibility to be taken lightly and for the treasure to be appreciated and desired requires as much understanding of situation as can be achieved.

The cases cited above have this in common: that those whose ministry is illustrated in them take seriously the context within which the gospel is to be shared. They live and work in the places and among the people who are their neighbours, their colleagues and their friends and they see them as such and not as targets or markets. They spend time, often years, understanding how to tend to the wellbeing of individuals, families and communities before advancing new initiatives and projects.

Sharing the gospel comes from the common life of a Christian community and is not primarily the action of individuals alone. The life of a local church or of other forms of Christian community is the seedbed and without the nurture, critique and encouragement that comes from mutuality, the gospel so easily becomes no more than an expression of individual desires or at worst neuroses.

The life of a local church consists of a number of components that might be characterized as: praying and worshipping, caring for one another, learning and growing in faith, sharing our faith and working for social justice. Each of these contributes to the way in which a Christian community is shaped and impacts in turn on the way in which the gospel is shared with others. Sharing the gospel comes best from those who do so from confidence and trust in God, not from fear of the other. It comes best from those who engage fully with the richness of their local context and culture.

Sharing the gospel with people and communities of other faiths is a challenge and an opportunity that must be understood in a humble spirit. Not only are individuals to be regarded as of equal value and worth as children of God and created in God's image, but their religious or other beliefs are not to be discounted or treated lightly or as of no worth. To disagree, and to disagree profoundly with someone, is not a licence to disparage or to demean. The history of relations between religions and cultures and the all-too-many hostile contemporary situations around the world mean that we come to encounters with others not in a neutral environment but in one that may be highly charged by views drawn from other parts of the world and other times. If there is proper opportunity in such encounter, there is also a challenge to a contrasting lukewarm-ness and lack of confidence.

In the cases illustrated, there is a deep concern to take seriously the human person whatever their religion or none – and to take religious beliefs seriously as an expression of a serious attempt to come before a God who is holy.

Sharing the gospel requires relationships of trust and indeed the processes of developing trust itself are themselves part of gospel sharing. Without trust, there will always be suspicion and a sense of being used for some other purpose. Our society is an anxious one in which mistrust of motive is now deeply rooted. Trust is created through personal human encounter, often in the simplest human activities of conversation about the ordinary things of life, through sharing of food and through little gestures of kindness and appreciation. Trust is created by openness and transparency and the avoidance of poor communication especially where tensions are created by other surrounding issues.

In several of the case studies warm personal relations had developed between leaders in the different communities and in the public authorities which had enabled tensions to be overcome and initiatives taken. The Church of England has a particular responsibility in this respect as a result of its role as the established Church and its presence in all communities. Many bishops have, for example, been entrusted with the work of convening the leadership of other faiths in their dioceses.

Sharing the gospel is rooted in the question of intent and motivation. We are commanded to always be 'prepared to give an answer to everyone who asks you to give the reason for the hope that you have'. But it is moderated both by the 'to everyone who asks you' and by the 'do it with gentleness and respect'. This implies not only a proper reticence, but also a question of motive. Gospel sharing should be motivated by a holistic concern for the wellbeing of the other and the wider community rather than by a personalized desire for the conversion of the other.

It is noticeable that in the cases cited, there is relatively little overt reference to evangelism or conversion and the language is, for example, of 'opportunities for creative expressions of the Christian story' and about 'how to engage effectively in the community and be a confident Christian presence' and these indicate something of the 'sensitive confidence' that best expresses the gospel way. In the end conversion is the work of the Holy Spirit, witness and proclamation is the work of the Church.

Appendix 1   Selected Reading List

Building good relations with people of other faiths, Inter Faith Network for the UK, 2003.

Dialogue and Inter-Religious Encounter, Inter Faith Network for the UK Mission, 1993.

'Christ and people of other faiths' and 'The way of dialogue' in *The Lambeth Conference 1988 – The truth shall make you free*, London: Church House Publishing, 1988.

The Church of England's Mission and Ministry in a Multi-Religious Society: Presence & Engagement Report 2017, Presence and Engagement Task Group, 2017. www.presenceandengagement.org.uk/sites/default/files/Report%20to%20General%20Synod%20July%202017.pdf (accessed 3 May 2019).

Presence & Engagement: The churches' task in a multi faith society, General Synod (GS 1577), 2005.

Board for Mission and Unity, *Towards a theology for inter-faith dialogue*, London: Church House Publishing, 1984.

David J. Bosch, *Transforming Mission: Paradigm Shifts in Theology of Mission*, Ossining, NY: Orbis, 1992.

Kenneth Cragg, *The Call of the Minaret*, Oxford: Oxford University Press, 1956.

David Goodhew (ed.), *Towards a Theology of Church Growth*, Farnham: Ashgate, 2015.

Michael Nazir-Ali, *The Unique and Universal Christ*, Milton Keynes: Paternoster Press, 2008.

Gerald O'Collins, *Jesus our redeemer: A Christian approach to salvation*, Oxford: Oxford University Press, 2007.

Gerald O'Collins, *Salvation for all: God's other peoples*, Oxford: Oxford University Press, 2008.

Cathy Ross and Colin Smith (eds), *Missional Conversations: A Dialogue between Theory and Praxis in World Mission*, Norwich: SCM Press, 2018.

Andrew Smith, *Vibrant Christianity in Multifaith Britain*, Abingdon: Bible Reading Fellowship, 2018.

Richard Sudworth, *Distinctly Welcoming: Christian presence in a multifaith society,* Scripture Union, 2007.

Theological Issues Consultative Group, *Christian Identity, Witness and Interfaith dialogue – a discussion document for the Decade of Evangelism*, CCBI Committee for relations with People of Other Faiths, 1991.

Andrew Wingate, *Celebrating Difference, Staying Faithful: How to Live in a Multi-faith World*, London: Darton Longman and Todd, 2005.

World Council of Churches, *Ecumenical considerations for dialogue and relations with people of other religions*, 2003. www.oikoumene.org/en/resources/documents/wcc-programmes/ interreligious-dialogue-and-cooperation/interreligious-trust-and -respect/ecumenical-considerations-for-dialogue-and-relations- with-people-of-other-religions [Accessed 3 May 2019]

Appendix 2 Existing Guidelines and Codes of Practice

Christian Witness in a Multi-Religious World, Recommendations for Conduct, World Council of Churches, World Evangelical Alliance, Pontifical Council for Interreligious Dialogue, 2011. Available from www.worldevangelicals.org/pdf/1106Christian_Witness_in_a_Multi-Religious_World.pdf.

Communities and Buildings: Church of England premises and other faiths, Inter Faith Consultative Group, 1996.

Dialogue and Evangelism among people of other faiths: principles for dialogue and evangelism, The Methodist Church, 1994. A Methodist reflection on the Inter Faith Network's Code of Conduct, adopted by the Methodist Conference in 1994 and published with a study guide in 1997.

Ethical Guidelines for Christian and Muslim Witness in Britain, Christian Muslim Forum, 2007.

Guidance on multi faith worship, Church of England House of Bishops, 1993.

Guidelines for the Celebration of Inter Faith Marriages, Inter Faith Consultative Group, 2004. Available from www.cofe.anglican.org/info/interfaith/marriageguidelines.

Guidelines for Inter Faith Marriages, Methodist Church, 2000. Adopted by the Methodist Conference of 2000.

In Good faith: The four Principles of Interfaith Dialogue – a brief guide for the Churches, CCBI Committee for Relations with People of Other Faiths, 1991.

Mission, Dialogue and Inter Religious Encounter, The Inter Faith Network UK, 1991.

Multi-Faith Worship?, Inter Faith Consultative Group, 1992.

Presence and Engagement Guidelines:
> *Use of Church Buildings,* 2017.
> *Baptism,* 2017.
> *Marriage.*
> *Schools: Hospitality.*
> *Civic Services.*
> Siriol Davies, *Shared Prayer Spaces.*
> Dr Andrew Smith, *Actions in Times of Tension.*
> The Revd Dr Tom Wilson, School: *Practical Issues*

Full list available from http://presenceandengagement.org.uk/content/resources?field_resource_type_tid=12.

Relations with People of other Faiths: Guidelines on Dialogue in Britain, British Council of Churches, 1981.

Room for Religion: Shared Facilities for Religious Use, Inter Faith Consultative Group, 1998.

Clinton Bennett (ed.), *Invitation to Dialogue,* CCBI Committee for Relations with People of Other Faiths, 1989.

Bishop of Bradford and Deobandi Association of Muslim Scholars in Britain, *Guidelines to Encourage Co-operation between Mosques & Churches, Imams & Clergy,* 2008. Available from http://presenceandengagement.org.uk/sites/default/files/Inter%20Faith%20Dialogue%20-%20Guidelines%20Between%20Mosques%20%26%20Churches.pdf.

Faith and Order Committee, *Use of Church Premises by People of Other Faiths,* Methodist Church, 1997. Adopted by the Methodist Conference of 1997.

Inter Faith Consultative Group of the Archbishops' Council, *Sharing One Hope?: the Church of England and Christian Jewish relations,* Church House Publishing, 2001.

Christopher Lamb ed., *Marriages between Christians and Muslims: pastoral guidelines for Christians and churches in Europe,* CCBI Committee for Relations with People of Other Faiths, 1998.

Porvoo Communion Consultation on Inter Faith Relations, *Guidelines for Inter Faith Encounter in the Churches of the Porvoo Communion,* 2003. Available from www.porvoocommunion.org/resources/general-resources/ (accessed 3 May 2019).

Roman Catholic Bishops' Conference of England and Wales, *Meeting God in Friend and Stranger,* The Catholic Truth Society, 2009.

Theological Issues Consultative Group, *Christian Identity, Witness and Interfaith dialogue – a discussion document for the Decade of Evangelism,* CCBI Committee for relations with People of Other Faiths, 1991.

Appendix 3   Christian-Muslim Forum: Ethical Evangelism guidelines

As members of the Christian Muslim Forum we are deeply committed to our own faiths (Christianity and Islam) and wish to bear faithful witness to them.

As Christians and Muslims we are committed to working together for the common good. We recognize that both communities actively invite others to share their faith and acknowledge that all faiths have the same right to share their faith with others.

There are diverse attitudes and approaches among us which can be controversial and raise questions. This paper is not a theology of Christian evangelism or mission or Da'wah (invitation to Islam), rather it offers guidelines for good practice.

The Christian Muslim Forum offers the following suggestions that, we hope, will equip Christians and Muslims (and others) to share their faith with integrity and compassion for those they meet.

- We bear witness to, and proclaim our faith not only through words but through our attitudes, actions and lifestyles.
- We cannot convert people, only God can do that. In our language and methods we should recognize that people's choice of faith is primarily a matter between themselves and God.

- Sharing our faith should never be coercive; this is especially important when working with children, young people and vulnerable adults. Everyone should have the choice to accept or reject the message we proclaim and we will accept people's choices without resentment.
- While we might care for people in need or who are facing personal crises, we should never manipulate these situations in order to gain a convert.
- An invitation to convert should never be linked with financial, material or other inducements. It should be a decision of the heart and mind alone.
- We will speak of our faith without demeaning or ridiculing the faiths of others.
- We will speak clearly and honestly about our faith, even when that is uncomfortable or controversial.
- We will be honest about our motivations for activities and we will inform people when events will include the sharing of faith.
- While recognizing that either community will naturally rejoice with and support those who have chosen to join them, we will be sensitive to the loss that others may feel.
- While we may feel hurt when someone we know and love chooses to leave our faith, we will respect their decision and will not force them to stay or harass them afterwards.

'Good News for Everyone? Evangelism and Other Faiths':

Deo Gloria Trust Lecture for the London School of Theology *13 March 2019, Lambeth Palace*

Thank you to the trustees of the Deo Gloria Trust for giving me the honour of delivering this year's lecture on evangelism. May I add my own warm welcome to the staff and friends of London School of Theology, and to Ruwani Gunawardene, who I know has worked so hard to make this evening's event happen. I apologize for the cold in here. If you fall asleep – well don't.

On becoming Archbishop of Canterbury I hoped to support the Five Marks of Mission of the Anglican Communion and the Quinquennial Goals of the Church of England over this phase of the Church's life by giving special priority to: prayer and the renewal of the religious life in community, reconciliation, and evangelism. I suspected at the time that the priority of evangelism would produce the most mixed response. For some, there would be high-fives and celebration, but for others perhaps a look of horror, and a response of 'Here we go again': yet another Christian leader pushing a recruitment drive!

The starting point for any treatment of evangelism must have nothing to do with any presumed evangelical tribalism, and everything to do with the heart of the Christian faith. In Christ Jesus, the whole of humanity is offered the gift of life with God, overcoming and transforming all the mess that we call sin. All that we know of God-in-Christ, however partial, however much a tiny foretaste of what is to be revealed, has implications not just for me, but every single person on this planet. There are two foundational principles here: the centrality of the person and work of Jesus Christ, and the universal offer of salvation through Christ. The history of the Church being embedded in different cultures and languages reflects a story that makes a difference in time and place; where history is interrupted by God's free gift to every one of us. I speak as someone who made a very clear decision to respond to God's free gift of salvation. I may be Archbishop of Canterbury but I've not always been into this world of Christian faith. On 12 October 1975, just before midnight, I prayed a prayer that changed my whole life. I remember saying to God, 'I don't know much if anything about you, but please come into my life and take charge.' I knew I faced a fork in the road: a decision to go one way, or another, and I knew that it had huge repercussions for me. I wasn't doing something that was merely about my personal comfort; a kind of private, spiritual lifestyle choice. This decision was about public truth. Words like justice, love, mercy would take on new meaning and weight because of Jesus Christ. Following Jesus Christ would be the business of public truth.

The famous Russian Orthodox scholar Vladimir Lossky has this lovely phrase: 'Jesus was the first fully human being.' In Jesus, I had begun to see how I ought to be, and how the world ought to be. Seeing the truth of who Christ is somehow connects us with the grain of the universe even in the midst of continued failings and struggles. That first tentative prayer, but clear decision in 1975, following the witness of friends at university, their prayers, their listening to me, and the patient discussions we had late at night, was a response to the transforming love of Christ; a gift offered to all of us.

Now I'm in that odd band of professional Christians, I'm no less aware that the salvation offered to me in Christ is free. It's a gift. I did not earn it and I never could. As it says in Romans 6, 'The free gift of God is eternal life in Christ Jesus our Lord.' That's not just life in the hereafter but it's participation in God's kingdom life of justice and peace on earth here and now. I didn't deserve any of this but through all the ups and downs, and, at times, the cost, it was the best decision I ever made. It's the best decision anyone could make, and it is exactly the same for everyone, clergy, Archbishops, criminals (sometimes the same), anyone. Sounds like good news, doesn't it?

Well this is where we get to the red meat of our lecture title: is evangelism really good news for everyone; and especially those of other faiths? I'm told that IT professionals have this acronym for what they regard as ideal system designs: 'WYSIWYG'. What You See Is What You Get. It's a good lesson for the Church: WYSIWYG: what you see is what you get. This good news is free, undeserved, a sheer gift from God available to all. The word evangelism from the Greek, literally means 'good news'. When we make our evangelism a product in a marketplace or an expression of cultural superiority, then we are falling short of the message given to us. Indeed, it is possible to embark upon evangelism in a way that denies and even contradicts the very one we proclaim. If it is free and undeserved, then there should be no place for coercion, for imperialistic ambition, for bait-and-switch techniques that buy people into the Church. Those practices are decidedly Bad News!

We would do well to heed the words of 1 Peter 3.15: 'Always be ready to make your defence to anyone who demands from you an account of the hope that is in you; yet do it with gentleness and reverence. Keep your conscience clear, so that, when you are maligned, those who abuse you for your good conduct in Christ may be put to shame.' We need to be ready: ready to speak, to share. This is hope for the world! But let that witness be seasoned with gentleness and respect. And let our actions of love, compassion, respect, gentleness confirm this as good news not bad news!

It was Marshall McLuhan that came up with that truism, 'the medium is the message'. Our evangelism, our witness, needs to reflect the message of salvation in Christ: the generous, universal gift; otherwise we are betraying the message entrusted to us. That our message calls us to certain standards is not lost on those of other faiths because all too often the Church has been bad news. This is where I'd like to suggest several challenges as we think about the business of evangelism in our current context of religious diversity.

The first challenge I wish to make is one to our Christian Ethics. In working out 'how then should we live?' there are a whole host of situations that we face where we have no prescriptive guide of what to do. In Christian freedom, we are called to pray, to worship, to read the Bible, celebrate the eucharist and be accountable to each other in the Church. Out of these repeated disciplines, we seek to live as Christ would have us live in the world. One key indicator of our ethical lives together as Christians comes from what has become known as the 'golden rule'. In Matthew 7.12, Jesus exhorts his followers 'in everything do to others as you would have them do to you, for this is the law and the prophets'. Have you ever been in a situation where someone has tried to persuade you of something without listening to anything you have said, not caring about your own experiences, and, what's more, spent most of the time belittling your views? I'd like to suggest that one of the most effective ways for Christians to learn about ethical evangelism is for us to experience what it is like to be witnessed to by someone of another faith in ways that don't seem to respect our own integrity or freedom, so we can then recognize where Christians sometimes act in parallel ways.

If you haven't experienced this first hand, then I would encourage you to use some imaginative process of empathy that might shape the practice of our evangelism.

In 2009, the Christian-Muslim Forum agreed a text suggesting how both communities could share their faith with mutual respect and understanding. Islam is another tradition that believes it has universal application and so Muslims are committed to their equivalent of evangelism: 'da'wah'. The guidelines for witness acknowledged that we could freely hold contrasting claims with universal implication, but that putting ourselves in the other's shoes would help us do this with genuine respect. As well as rejecting coercion and inducements, one of the guidelines asserts that 'We will speak of our faith without demeaning or ridiculing the faith of others'. This is a big statement but it's based on the golden rule: would I want to have a discussion about my Christian faith, what is most precious to me, if the other person spent their time ridiculing my faith? I would want to know the other person was listening to me and taking me seriously. If I would want that, then I should give that freedom to others.

In the Anglican Church Calendar, we remember Sadhu Sundar Singh. He was an Indian follower of Christ, living the itinerant life of a holy man at the beginning of the twentieth century. Sundar Singh had known the transforming power of Christ Jesus and wanted to tell others about Jesus. He would tell stories that represented his understanding of this free gift. One such story that speaks to the heart of our ethics of evangelism is of a man in a dark house. This man can see only by the light of a candle. Sundar Singh said, 'Do we quench the candle, or do we open the doors and the windows to let in the light of the sun?' Let us never be guilty of demeaning the light that others have; just show them something of the light you know. Let's tell people about Jesus and witness to what he has done for us, without feeling the need to presume to tell others what is wrong with their faith.

This moves us on to the second challenge, and that is to truly listen to the person of another faith in our witness. Another aspect of 'the medium is the message', of What You See Is What You Get, is the incarnational nature of the Christian faith. God, in Christ, enters into the life of the world in time and place. God has entered, irreversibly, into the hopes and dreams of his creation: the salvation story is one shot through with dialogue. The Word doesn't just speak, but listens! Here's where I want to share something of the 'Gospel According to Pixar'.

In the film, *The Incredibles*, the villain, Syndrome, has Mr Incredible, our erstwhile hero, trapped, and begins to talk him through his motivations, 'Now you respect me, because I'm a threat. That's the way it works. Turns out there are lots of people, whole countries, that want respect, and will pay through the nose to get it. How do you think I got rich? I invented weapons, and now I have a weapon that only I can defeat, and when I unleash it …' At this point, Mr Incredible tries to escape, and then Syndrome says, 'You sly dog! You got me monologuing!' It's a humorous take on a commonplace convention in adventure films where the villain shows off while the hero tries to keep him talking until he works out a way to get out of the fix he is in. Let's be honest. How much of our evangelism is monologuing? Speaking irrelevantly to those who may as well not be there, and if they did get a word in edge ways, it would make no difference whatsoever to what we were saying anyway. Becky Pippert puts it well when she says: 'Evangelism is not memorizing techniques to use on unsuspecting victims.' Evangelism and dialogue are not opposites. Any credible witness requires us to be in dialogue with the other; to hear the hopes, fears, and experiences of the person of another faith. Any dialogue with the faith other should involve us in witnessing to our hope in Christ, and doing so with both ears as well as one mouth.

If we are truly listening to the person of another faith, then one of the things we are likely to hear is something of the legacy of colonialism and the Western Church's complicity in that. It's something that I know I need to be especially alive to as a white man of a certain age, who happens to be an Archbishop in the established Church of England. We've got form! It's another aspect of that requirement of empathy; of being able to listen. But the third challenge is the need to be conscious of our colonial history and how it has impacted other faiths in Britain today. How are British Christians heard when we talk of the claims of Christ by diaspora communities who have experienced abuse and exploitation by an empire that has seemed to hold the Christian story at the heart of its project? Remember our starting point of the good news of the free gift of salvation to us in Christ? Remember that this free gift is given to us undeserving, meaning that no one is entitled or better. The ideology underlying the British Empire, make no mistake, was largely predicated on the superiority of the British. The Church often colluded with that, and it was a thoroughly un-Christian worldview.

A number of my colleagues here at Lambeth Palace have recently come back from India. As part of that trip, they visited the site of the notorious Jallianwala Bagh massacre in Amritsar. In 1919, hundreds of Indians were killed by the British Army while publicly and peaceably gathering to celebrate a local festival. The machine gun magazines that were emptied on innocent men, women and children have left indelible marks on the remains of buildings in the park, the site of the massacre, and on the consciousness of Indian Sikhs, Hindus and Muslims. Whether we like it or not, this atrocity, and so many others, was perpetrated by

Christians and done in the name of Christian Society. It's not good news; it's not of God; it's not Christ-like. So, how might our witness hear the concerns of people of other faiths that we might, instead, be embarking on another imperialistic and dehumanizing venture?

Some time ago, I heard that in one African country I know, the local Christians in what is a largely mixed Christian-Muslim area of the country discouraged a foreign, western Christian from coming to lead what he described publicly as an 'evangelistic crusade'. The local Christians knew the sensitivities of the communal relations and how charged that word 'crusade' was in the long history of Christian-Muslim relations. Against their advice, the crusade went ahead and hundreds were killed in subsequent riots. The errors and sins of the past are part and parcel of our present and we have a responsibility to be attentive to how that past colours the reception of our witness.

Let's remember, though, that the Christian message is not British, and it is not white, but it is for all. Therefore, and I stand here very aware of the strides that my own church needs to take on this matter, we need to be church communities that embody diversity. One of the evangelistic tasks for British people is to ensure that we point to a living vibrant faith and one that does not reflect the cultural assumptions of nominal allegiance. In global terms, a typical Anglican Christian is an African woman under the age of thirty living in poverty. In Britain, our most dynamic and fastest-growing churches are black-led churches with cultural roots that go back to Nigeria and Ghana. This gospel we proclaim is good news for everyone!

I read some recent research that suggested that nearly half of millennials (those in their 20s and 30s) believe that it is wrong to share their faith with someone of a different faith in the hope that someday they will share the same faith. What is revealing about this research is that those millennials are happy to talk of the centrality of Jesus Christ and adhere to mainstream orthodox beliefs. I believe that we need to take seriously the abuses of our history and engage other faiths with humility and empathy because our mandate to witness will otherwise be disowned by a younger generation much more attuned to necessary demands for respect and cultural diversity.

Part of an imperialistic approach to evangelism is a view that we come with our plenty to the benighted, suffering, living in darkness. My fourth challenge, and perhaps the one that those of us from the evangelical tradition find hardest, is that of being prepared to learn from someone of another faith. When we listen seriously to people of other faiths, we will find that many receive great solace from their tradition. We are not contradicting any of the claims we make about the centrality of Jesus Christ to the whole of creation, our commitment to him as the source of all salvation, by recognizing that other traditions offer people encouragement, community, and even deep wells of spirituality. But we may find our understanding challenged and enriched.

This is another aspect of us needing to listen. Max Warren, a celebrated Anglican missionary-scholar put it like this: 'Our first task in approaching another people, another culture, another religion is to take off our shoes, for the place we are approaching is holy. Else we may find ourselves treading on people's dreams. More serious still, we may forget that God was here before our arrival.' This is the essence of what we call the missio dei: the mission of God. God's mission of reconciliation goes before and beyond anything that we may see. Evangelism is not about dispensing bits of 'our' God that we hold in our pockets. While we can talk of the relationship we can have with God through our faith in Christ

Jesus, on one level of speaking, every single person is already the recipient of gifts of God. In that great hymn of praise to Christ Jesus in the first chapter of the letter to the Colossians, we have these words, 'He is the image of the invisible God, the firstborn of all creation, for in him all things in heaven and on earth were created ... all things have been created through him and for him. He is himself before all things, and in him all things hold together.'

St Augustine said, 'God is closer to us than we are to ourselves.' For those of Christian faith, other faith, and no faith, where does every act of love and justice and kindness come from but God-in-Christ? I hope that what I'm going to say now is not controversial: some people outside the church are more like Jesus than some people in it! All that is good, true and beautiful comes from God. This should be no surprise, nor embarrassment. And as Christians we want to name the source of all that is good, true and beautiful as Christ Jesus and help people connect with that life-giving source and end of all our being, that they may be in covenant relationship with God. But it means that the encounter with someone who is not a Christian, and indeed professes another faith altogether, is still an encounter that can lead me into meeting Christ afresh: to receiving a gift of God from that other person.

As I share the love of Christ with someone of another faith, witnessing to the transformation that he brings and that good news that is freely available to all, what in that other person may reveal to me something of Christ that I don't know yet? Think of the story of the Good Samaritan. It is NOT a story about being nice to people not like you. It is the story of the person not like you showing you what godly neighbourliness might look like: the person outside the fold of faith who reveals something of the love of God. Evangelism, in this spirit that I am outlining, is not a triumphant march of arrogance but a humble, generous journey of sharing and receiving.

I think of my friend Abdullah bin Bayyah, a Muslim scholar committed to non-violence and, to his cost, to Muslim societies that accept Christians worshipping in full freedom. His life has been an example to me: I do not hesitate to name his graciousness and spirituality as gifts from God. This recognition does not stop me from affirming that Jesus Christ is the revelation of God-with-us and that a decision to follow him is the best decision anyone can make. But the recognition of my Muslim friend's love and grace as a gift of God to me starts a genuine friendship.

In a recent book on interfaith relations, it talks of the need to balance persuasion with curiosity. This book agrees that evangelism should be on the table as part of transparent and honest exchanges between people of faith. The issue is not evangelism *per se*. We try to *persuade* or commend things to others all the time, and in lots of different ways. The issue is whether we treat the other person seriously or not, and this is expressed in our level of *curiosity*. If we want to persuade someone that Jesus is the answer to all their hopes and longings and yet we have no curiosity over their hopes and longings, nor how their religious tradition may even respond to those longings, then we are evidently not that interested in the other. How might our witness persuade and be persuasive, while also being genuinely curious about the other? This is not in the sense of finding the knock-down argument to defeat the other but in seeking out what is significant, how they tick, the uniqueness of their stories. As Max Warren said, the worst error would be in forgetting that God was here before our arrival. Our Bible reminds us of a rollcall of characters beyond the covenant household of God who became bearers of grace, even gifts to God's people: Rahab, Ruth, Cyrus, the

Syrophoenician woman, Cornelius. If evangelicals remind the whole church of our mandate to witness to salvation in Christ, maybe my liberal brothers and sisters remind me that there are those beyond the church, including those of other faiths, who may end up showing me something of the love of God.

This leads me to my final challenge. Treating people seriously and recognizing the image of God in the other and their eternal value to God means that we should never fall into the trap of evangelism as technique. This is about relationship, about love, not about building a power base. Evangelism isn't a tool of the Church, or about using God so we can still be here in a generation or two. How do we express our love for others in witness so that they understand that we care for them even if they make no decision to follow Christ? Christians need to know that we can be smelt a mile off if our agenda is one that reaches out to others only if they are interested in becoming Christians. In our world today, people are crying out for unconditional love: to be accepted in community. The Church should be the last place on earth that feels like you need a special passport or have to reach a particular entry requirement. Again, What You See Is What You Get should be our motto, so whoever you are, whatever language, culture, gender, age, ability, education, sexuality, job status, wealth etc, then you are welcome to share in God's good gifts. What do you think we communicate when we cosy up to someone because we think they may come to the church social or the Alpha course, they say no and we suddenly drop that burgeoning friendship? The message we relay is that they only have value to us if they become Christians. That doesn't reflect the free gift of God to us in Christ: made available to the whole world. Whether we are interested or not, near or far from God, God's initiative was freely made towards us.

Overlay that kind of conditional friendship-making with the cultural and religious histories of our nation and you can see the potentially toxic mix for relations with other faiths. This is why so many religious groups rightly complain of being 'targeted' by Christians. It's one thing to feel a calling to share your lives with a particular culture or people. It's another thing altogether to see their value only as would-be Christians.

Going back to those Christian-Muslim communities in Africa that I mentioned, these were churches that were witnessing daily in shared lives as friends and neighbours. They would have to continue as friends and neighbours long after the foreign missionary finished his evangelistic crusade. Witnessing to the claims of Christ, sharing what we know of that salvation story, comes in the midst of everyday stuff where we are called to speak, and where our deeds are meant to back up our words. It's for this reason that the Church of England's programme to resource our engagement with other faiths is called 'Presence and Engagement'. Those words were chosen deliberately to represent the full range of ways we might connect with people of other faiths in our communities – through neighbourly service, dialogue, witness and shared action for the common good. Some people are fond of quoting St Francis saying 'Preach the gospel at all times. When necessary, use words.' At risk of being controversial again, it is unlikely that St Francis said this and I'm not sure we should use this quotation as a get-out clause to avoid verbal witness. We are called to preach the gospel with our words, to testify, to witness to what God has done in Christ. Words are not the last resort. However, our words need to explain our deeds and our deeds support our words.

In a cathedral I know well, there has been extensive project work serving refugees from a largely Muslim faith background. It is a ministry involving advice and counselling, social contact, friendship and hosting. It's the kind of ministry replicated up and down the country in so many churches. It has been faithful, quiet, unassuming, and if the workers and volunteers were honest with you, they'd admit to a level of discomfort around this word 'evangelism'. Again, let's remember the ethical challenge of not offering inducements with evangelism. Their story is not about inappropriate inducements though but shared lives of faith. One of the joys in Britain becoming a much more multi cultural and multi faith country is that we are rubbing shoulders up against each other in profound ways and have the potential to offer mutual challenge and learning. Many other faith communities don't have the same queasiness around matters of faith that we sometimes do. Faith is not a forbidden topic of conversation to polite conversation at the dinner table along with politics and sex: the unconditional love of God is not a privatized lifestyle choice, it is public truth. The cathedral workers and volunteers are beginning to learn to respond to the questions of refugees wanting to learn more about the Christian faith: giving an account of the hope that is within them. Intertwined in these conversations are stories of dreams and visions, prayerful searches, because the refugees are familiar with the supernatural and the significance of prayer.

Somehow, in the providence of God, witnessing to Christ, offering good news that is genuinely good news, rebounds in a virtuous circle where we too may meet Christ afresh. Witnessing to the gift of Christ is an intrinsic part of our calling. However, faithful witness will lead us into and spring from friendship, partnership, and wonder, as well as the joys of others discovering Christ anew alongside those of other religious traditions. In many other places around the world, this is a path that is costly, where the ultimate price is paid. The privilege of living in a free and mature democracy is that we can both be held accountable to what we do and what we profess, while enjoying the freedom to pray expectantly and to speak intentionally of what we know of the transforming love of Christ Jesus. The challenges I have suggested are no guarantee that we will not face rejection or even opposition. But let us face rejection and opposition for being faithful, not because we were unethical, monologuing, imperialistic, arrogant or unloving.

We are called to speak, to witness, to share, but the work of the Holy Spirit in the lives of others will always be a mystery to us. That is why we need to witness in dialogue; in genuine humility. I heard of one parish priest even this last week who was preaching to his congregation, boosted unexpectedly in recent years by those baptized and confirmed from other faith backgrounds. He challenged them with those words of Jesus in John 15: 'You did not choose me but I chose you.' The priest acknowledged the very different routes his congregation had taken to get there: in some cases literally by boat, and smuggled in lorries. He acknowledged that some had met a Christian who had given them a Bible back in their home country, some had had dreams and visions of Jesus, or had been beguiled by stories of Jesus even from within their own religious tradition. Still others had had very mixed motives when they began attending the church, enjoying the community and support that the church offered but ambivalent about the Christian faith. At each of these stages, the priest said, God, by his Holy Spirit, was drawing them to himself, calling each of them. Our part in that story of God's reconciliation with humanity is one that means that evangelism is not about conquest or competition, still less about survival and saving the church. But it is about confident yet humble witnessing to good news to all. Jesus Christ is good news; let's not become bad news to those of other faiths.

Archbishop Justin Welby